Biopower, Racism, State Racism and The Modern/
Post Modern North Atlantic State

Michel Foucault's Genealogy of the
Historico-Political Discourse of Race War
Deconstructed

Daurius Figueira

Table of Contents

Introduction

The twenty-first century has produced the return of white racist discourse to positions of power in the politics of the North Atlantic. Where white supremacist political solutions and actions are being proffered and operationalised in the politics of the North Atlantic. The twenty-first century discourse of white supremacy is framed by a paranoia fed siege mentality, generated by grave threats posed to white civilisation and hegemony of various types and origins, with a penchant for extremism. The most potent threat articulated as it resonates with electorates is the threat posed by the non-white, non-Christian hordes seeking to swamp white, Christian citadels of hegemony, civilisation, identity and lineage/DNA. The white race in their ancestral homelands are being threatened with becoming mongrelised and losing their demographic dominance. The explanations made of this reality are dismal failures as they cannot expose the link racism has to power relations, politics, the State and the maintenance of the hierarchy of the social order in the North Atlantic. They only speak of racism as a personal infection, a transactional instrument and a remnant from a past historical epoch existing in a powerless void in the social order. Its use in political mobilisation is simply to win elections sustainably as those elected to office are not hard-core ideologues just political opportunists, hence "populists" where "liberal democracy" will ultimately prevail. Others speak of racism as a reality and stress its negative impact, but are silent on its nexus with power relations. The gross failure of the "scientific" fields/disciplines to expose the reality of racism demands a return to the works of Michel Foucault in search of an explanation. For explanations forwarded from the Enlightenment project have proven to be hollow as it simply cannot expose the nexus between racism and power, power relations and the State.

In his 1976 public lecture at the College de France Michel Foucault presented his genealogy of a historico-political discourse of Europe from the seventeenth to the twentieth centuries, specifically in the context of Britain and France. In the course of presenting his genealogy Foucault gave insights into the nexus between racism and the development of this historico-political discourse over time in Europe. Foucault mentioned the impact of racism formulated and operationalised under the European racist colonial imperial enterprise and its impact on the evolution of European metropolitan racist discourse. Foucault's most potent analysis presented dealt with the formulation of bourgeois discourse in the nineteenth century and thereafter towards establishing bourgeois discursive hegemony in Europe. Foucault identified a specific technology of power of bourgeois discourse that operationalised the biopolitics of this hegemonic discourse which is biopower, where power focuses on the biology of the species towards establishing and maintaining hegemony through the power relations of biology/biopolitics, where the body is now the focus of politics. Foucault in his description of biopower reveals the vital operational nexus between racism and biopower where racism, specifically white supremacy, empowers the State form generated by biopower to be a murderous State. This biopower State is a racist State as it practices State racism. The biopolitics of the twentieth century North Atlantic State is then rooted in two technologies of power that operationalise racism in order to police the social order. They are racist States that operationalise State racism in order to maintain the power relations/ hierarchy of the social order. This has nothing to do with being racist, this is simply a reality at the local level; but at the State level, at the political level, racism is a vital operational mechanism that ensures the integrity of the social order of the North Atlantic. Racism, white supremacy is organic to the existential condition of the modern and post-modern North Atlantic State.

The impact of a public political discourse of racism with discursive characteristics paralleling that of National Socialism and Fascism in the politics of the North Atlantic in the twenty-first century indicates that biopolitics/ biopower and the technologies of power have now reawakened, operationalised and deployed a specific discourse of white supremacy, which is a white supremacist, racist, paranoid, militarist, discourse. This is a racist discourse expressing grave paranoia over fear of a black planet that is threatening to immerse and pollute white citadels of race identity, culture, civilisation and most importantly racial lineage/DNA. This is a discourse that was first formulated in the slave colonies of Europe in the West Indies in the eighteenth and nineteenth centuries where the white oligarchs, especially the slave owners, were the minority and the enslaved Africans the majority. Where this white oligarchy lived on a day to day basis in expectation of the white genocide at the hands of the Africans which generated the fear of a black planet. The Haitian Revolution of 1804 drove this discourse into overdrive where public spectacles of brutality were the chosen vehicle to keep the salient threat at bay. This racist paranoia adopted knee jerk solutions of graphic brutality to stymie the perceived threat of white genocide. But this racist paranoia destroyed the capacity of the capitalist enterprise hinged on enslavement for the production of raw sugar for export to be a viable wealth generation unit. This is the racist paranoid discourse that is now being hinted and gestures point to in the "populist" politics of the North Atlantic. This is not a neo-Nazi or neo-fascist flashback, it is a reversion to, a resurrection of a racist paranoid West Indian discourse of slavery. To this end I have included a deconstruction of two instances of this discourse in the text.

In the Course Summary of the 1976 public lecture Foucault states: "we have to look at how relations of subjugation can manufacture subjects." "and if we have to think of power in terms of relations of force, do we therefore have to interpret it in terms of the general form of war? Can war serve as an analyser of power relations?" (Foucault 2003 pgs. 265-266). Foucault insists that power must be conceptualised in terms of relations of force/relations of subjugation which raise the question of how subjects of power are manufactured? Power conceptualised as force then raises the question of war as an instrument to analyse power relations in the social order. Foucault states: "But the first question that has to be asked is perhaps this: How, when, and in what way did people begin to imagine that it is war that functions in power relations, that an uninterrupted conflict undermines peace, and that the civil order is basically an order of battle." (Foucault 2003 pg. 267). The answer to this question lies in the discursive constructs of the historico-political discourse Foucault presents a genealogy of in 1976. The questions that drive and in turn limit the expanse of the 1976 lecture are for Foucault as follows: "How did people begin to perceive a war just beneath the surface of peace? Who tried to find the principle that explained order, institutions, and history in the noise and confusion of war and in the mud of battles? Who was the first to think that war was the continuation of politics by other means?" (Foucault 2003 pg. 267). In the

4

course of constructing a genealogy of this historico-political discourse framed by this series of questions Foucault discovers the link between European racism and this discourse which further evolves into the link between European racist discourse, European colonial derived racist discourse and European hegemonic discourse. Which came to fruition in the nineteenth to the twentieth centuries in hegemonic European discourse with its technology of biopower rooted in biopolitics deploying racism as an instrument of biopower creating the nexus: biopower, racism and State racism. This is Foucault's greatest and gravest revelation in his genealogy presented in 1976 for in the twenty-first century the nexus continues and has evolved. This is the link between power, power relations and racism in the North Atlantic revealed. This is racism as an instrument of power utilised to classify into typologies and police populations, to be part of the mechanism of power that constitutes subjects of power. Racism is organic to power and together they constitute State racism in the North Atlantic in the twenty-first century as it was in the nineteenth and twentieth centuries. The modern and post-modern North Atlantic state is a racist State.

Chapter One
Foucault's Public Lecture 1976
War, Politics and Power

From January 1976 to March 1976 Michel Foucault presented his public lecture at the College de France for the year 1976. In this lecture Foucault chose to expand on his discourse of power and power relations published in English as "Discipline and Punish" prior to the 1976 lecture. Foucault would present a discursive theme on power and power relations in the 1976 lecture which he never devoted a book to or returned to in a subsequent public lecture. This discursive theme deals specifically with an approach to studying power/force relations in the European social order which is a signal instrument of Foucault's anti-Enlightenment discourse and powerfully revealing of the masked reality of European and North Atlantic power. As a voyager in the journey to escape colonial and neo-colonial arrested development this most potent instrument unleashed by Foucault in 1976, and thereafter discarded, afforded me the ability to unmask the discursive genesis of the European and North Atlantic colonial and neo-colonial order which lies at the heart of the European and North Atlantic social order. In 1976 Foucault then unleashed the greatest gift he afforded those of us of the neo-colonial order to deconstruct the discursive order of Europe and the North Atlantic that refuses, from the fifteenth century to 2018, to walk away from its racist, colonial, imperialist worldview driven by the quest for hegemony.

Foucault defines his 1976 project as follows: "and if we have to think of power in terms of relations of force, do we therefore have to interpret it in terms of the general form of war? Can war serve as an analysis of power relations?" (Foucault 2003 pg.266). Foucault continues: "But the first question that has to be asked is perhaps this: How, when, and in what way did people begin to imagine that it is war that functions in power relations, that an uninterrupted conflict undermines peace, and that the civil order is basically an order of battle?" (Foucault 2003 pg.266). Foucault then states the specific questions that have been posed in the 1976 lecture the nature of which indicate that this

6

was a project that Foucault never returned to towards publishing a study of. Following the 1976 lecture Foucault began the series on sexuality which filled his last three books. The specific questions posed then indicate that in 1976 he was in fact presenting a genealogy of the discourse of the social order as an order of battle. Foucault states: "How did people begin to perceive a war just beneath the surface of peace? Who tried to find the principle that explained order, institutions, and history in the noise and confusion of war and in the mud of battles? Who was the first to think that war is the continuation of politics by other means? (Foucault 2003 pg.267) My task has been to apply this limited presentation of Foucault towards deconstructing the European discourse of the social order as an order of battle towards exposing the nature of the social order of the North Atlantic. This has now afforded insights into the European colonial order which was an order of battle and the neo colonial order of former British colonies. Most of all Foucault has afforded an instrument to deconstruct the genesis, evolution and persistence of European and North Atlantic racism.

Session One: 7 January 1976

Subjugated Knowledges, Genealogy, Archaeology

Foucault introduces in this session the discursive concept of subjugated knowledges. Subjugated knowledges are disqualified, rejected and discarded discourses by dint of the fact they are non-hegemonic, local as they are the discourses of those constituted by power, the subjects of power and the effects of power/knowledge. As the body and mind is the terrain upon which hegemonic discourse acts to constitute the subject of power/knowledge the subject of power/knowledge produces a subjugated discourse that is banished by hegemonic discourse by dint of the threat it poses to hegemonic discourse. There are then power/force relations that impact the human subject/object of power/ knowledge and the discourse of the human subject/object of power. There are power/force relations and the dynamic of force relations which are animated by resistance and struggle at play at the level of the body, mind and discourse. This environment of force relations encompasses the micro to the macro levels from the actions and discourse of the single individual to the macro level which is the pressing need for an architecture of power/force relations that contain, embrace and place limits to the dynamic of the force relations in Europe, it's called the State. Foucault states: "I am also referring to a whole series of knowledges that have been disqualified as nonconceptual knowledges, as insufficiently elaborated knowledges: naïve knowledges, hierarchically inferior knowledges, knowledges that are below the required level of erudition or scientificity." (Foucault 2003 pg.7). These subjugated knowledges are then inferior to scientific knowledge and they are subjugated because of their inferiority. A condition which exceeds the conventional explanation that the discourse exercising hegemony branded them inferior according to the discourse of truth of scientific discourse. Science then is the weapon used to assault and exercise hegemony over those targeted for domination. Science is then simply a discourse of truth where truth is manufactured in the service of science, domination and hegemony. Foucault states: "And it is thanks to the reappearance of these knowledges from below, of these unqualified or disqualified knowledges: the knowledge of the psychiatrised, the patient, the nurse, the doctor, that is parallel to, marginal to, medical knowledge, the knowledge of the delinquent, what I would call, if you like, what people know (and this is by no means the same thing as common knowledge or common sense but, on the contrary a particular knowledge, a knowledge that is local, regional, or differential, incapable of unanimity and which derives its power solely from the fact that it is different from all the knowledges that surround it), it is the reappearance of what people know at a local level, of these disqualified knowledges, that made the critique possible." (Foucault 2003 pgs. 7-8). The resistance of these disqualified knowledges to hegemonic scientific discourse, the pushing up from below makes possible Foucault's anti-Enlightenment, anti-science project. As the basis of assault on hegemonic scientific discourse is the disqualified knowledges but what is vitally necessary is an instrument of antisciences, an instrument that enables, prompts and facilitates an insurrection of knowledges. Knowledges locked in a power relation with the hegemonic scientific discourses seeking to reverse the hegemony scientific discourses exert towards creating a new power/force relation as the human can never be emancipated from power/force relations. Revolution is then a myth of scientific discourse as it wills into existence the mask of repression as an explanatory tool. For Foucault Genealogy is the antiscience and Archaeology its methodology. Foucault states: "Genealogies, are quite specifically, antisciences. They are about the insurrection of knowledges. Genealogy has to fight the power-effects characteristic of any discourse that is regarded as scientific." (Foucault 2003 pg.9). Foucault continues as follows: "genealogy is, then, a sort of attempt to desubjugate historical knowledges, to set them free, or in other words to enable them to oppose and struggle against the coercion of a unitary, formal and, scientific theoretical discourse. The project of these disorderly and tattered genealogies is to reactivate local knowledges-...against the scientific hierarchicalisation of knowledge and its intrinsic power-effects." (Foucault 2003 Pg. 10). The first order is the choice of historical knowledges as the basis of the assault on the hegemony of scientific discourse which means that subjugated historical knowledges have to be desubjugated via genealogy. Genealogies will then engage with the power-effects of scientific discourse but the crux of the matter is the concept of "power -effects." Power has to be strategic, it has to be driven by an overarching strategy in order for it to impact its target with "effects." All power is then strategic and it begets resistance and it is operational within a field of struggle which entails power relations. Power is then joined to effects as it's to knowledge towards constituting its ideal individual placed in a social order which is the prime expression of the strategic relational context of power. Genealogy assaults the strategic order of power-effects and power/knowledge by falsifying the operational scientific discourse that is driving the strategic power instance. Genealogy strips power bare, naked impacting the operational stability of power-effects. Foucault continues: "Archaeology is the method specific to the analysis of local discursivities, and genealogy is the tactic which, once it has described these local discursivities, brings into play the desubjugated knowledges that have been released from them. That just about sums up the overall project." (Foucault 2003 pgs. 10-11). You locate the local discourses, then you mine them with the archaeological method or discourse mining and finally you deploy the strategic tactic of genealogy where the emancipated former subjugated knowledges will now be utilised to assault the power-effects and power/knowledge instruments of hegemonic scientific discourse. The discourse miner can then evolve into a discursive agent responsible for formulating discursive lines and structures rooted in desubjugated knowledges with a strategic objective and its instruments to engage with hegemonic discourse in the quest for hegemony. Foucault states: "The way things stand, the fragments of genealogy that have been done are in fact still there, surrounded by a wary silence." "The silence, or rather the caution with which unitary theories avoid the genealogy of knowledge might therefore be one reason for going on." (Foucault 2003 pg. 12). I can attest to this reality with my experiences as a post-graduate student in Sociology and Government and as a member of academic staff of a university. In my case the silence masked a strategy of power to destroy my academic and post graduate careers. Which flows with the following position of Foucault as follows: "Given that we are talking about a battle-the battle knowledges are waging against the power-effects of scientific discourse-." (Foucault 2003 pg. 12). Foucault's project of genealogy is based on and rooted in historical knowledges which explains the content and focus of his 1976 public lecture. In the 1976 public lecture Foucault presented a genealogy of a specific historical knowledge of the European social order: the discourse of race war.

Power and War

Foucault at this juncture begins his presentation in the first session on power. Foucault states that European scientific discourses on power have put forward the following: "if power is indeed the implementation and deployment of a relationship of force, rather than analysing it in terms of surrender, contract, and alienation or rather than analysing it in functional terms as the reproduction of the relations of production, shouldn't we be analysing it first and foremost in terms of conflict, confrontation, and war?" (Foucault 2003 pg. 15). Foucault now presents two hypotheses: the hypothesis of power is repression and the hypothesis of power is war. This second hypothesis conjures up a whole new worldview but is it hegemonic? Foucault states: "Power is war, the continuation of war by other means." He continues as follows: "Politics, in other words, sanctions and reproduces the disequilibrium of forces manifested in war." "within this 'civil peace', these political struggles, these clashes over or with power, these modifications of relations of force...in a political system, all these things must be interpreted as a continuation of war." (Foucault 2003 Pg. 16). The two hypotheses are not singular of each other for war begets repression they are supportive of each other's rationale as scientific hegemonic discourse. Foucault's grave dilemma in his formulation of a genealogical definition of power is apparent at this juncture in January 1976. In his formulation presented in History of Sexuality Volume 1 Foucault dumped both hypotheses, but in doing so he dumped the golden child with the bath water whose existence he revealed in the public lecture of 1976. Foucault in the closing stages of session 1 in 1976 gave glimpses of the golden child as emancipated knowledge who by his actions thereafter returned to being a subjugated knowledge. Foucault's position on the analysis of power is that an attempt to evade the economistic schemata the two grand hypotheses present themselves: the mechanism of power is repression and the basis of a power relationship is a clash between forces highly reminiscent of war and the battlefield. In the History of Sexuality Volume 1 it's obvious why Foucault dumped both grand hypotheses for a genealogy of sexuality demanded much more than repression, as a flowering of possibility under power to facilitate compliance was necessary. And the state of war in the politics of the social order fails to 'see' sexuality as a means of constituting willing subjects who police themselves, their sexuality included, for a state of war begets hard repression that has no place under the order of Biopolitics. In dumping the position that power relations reflect a state of war Foucault crippled the ability of his discourse to effectively lay bare the intricacies and contradictions of politics and the struggle for political dominance in the North Atlantic. In the actual game of North Atlantic politics Foucault's concept of power in History of Sexuality Volume 1 is of little relevance, which raises the question if power in the North Atlantic is multimodal even a shape shifter? And that all of the theorising forwarded in scientific discourse and the hard glimpses afforded by genealogy are simply describing specific faces/aspects/operational realities presented by power in its operational modes? Power is only what it is by contact/being exercised, it has and can have no other existence, then it's heavily defined by the contextual reality of all contact present, past and future in a quantum milieu. Foucault states: "I think that the twin notions of "repression" and "war" have to be considerably modified and ultimately, perhaps, abandoned." (Foucault 2003 pg. 17).

In the final words of his first session for 1976 Foucault reveals the golden child, later abandoned, as follows: "Then I will try to look again at the theory that war is the historical principle behind the workings of power, in the context of the race problem, as it was racial binarism that led the West to see for the first time that it was possible to analyse political power as war. And I will try to trace this down to the moment when race struggle and class struggle became, at the end of the nineteenth century, the two great schemata that were used to identify the phenomenon of war and the relationship of force within political society." (Foucault 2003 Pgs.18-19). The theory of political power as war flows from a discourse of the race problem, of racial binarism as the basis of the European social order. This river of discourse is then the discourse of race and race struggle and the theory of political power as war is simply one mechanism of power that flows from and to this river of race war and race struggle. This discursive river evolves with time and one such stage is when race struggle now becomes expressed as class struggle. The discourse of race struggle, race war constitutes the position that political power is war, it also absorbs class struggle and presents it as the new interpretation of the original duality, but this development cannot wipe away the other duality constituted and embraced by the discursive river before class struggle. This is the duality of the European, white male, inherently superior, the sole single recipient of manifest destiny juxtaposed with all non-white races of the world. This is the golden child. This discursive river constituted the race concept where the master race (white) juxtaposed to the inferior races of the world (black) and then determined that the power relations between the master and the inferiors is a race struggle, a race war. And the social order and all its institutions and mechanisms of power constituted where a minority of the master race is exercising hegemony over an inferior majority, then the social order is constructed on a race war footing to ensure the hegemony of the master race/ the minority. What then is the process of decolonisation when you implant North Atlantic political structures on this social order premised on the power relations of war? You have neo-colonial collapse. So-called European scientific racism is simply the casting of a "scientific" veneer over a non-scientific discourse that flows from the discursive river of race war, race struggle. Foucault was simply not interested in this golden child as it was irrelevant to his agenda as he was not the product of a failing neo-colonial social order, as I am. This is my interest and to unlock the edifice of hate both personal and for the "other" you need to journey through the discourse of Frantz Fanon. This present journey must now deconstruct Foucault's genealogy of the discourse of race war, race struggle.

Chapter Two
Session Three: 21 January 1976
Discourse of Race War

In this session Foucault presents his genealogy of the discourse of race war where he points out that almost immediately following the consolidation of the power of the State over war, which was accomplished through the creation of military institutions under the control of the State and the resultant professional army, the discourse appeared on the discursive landscape. Foucault states: "A new discourse, a strange discourse. It was new, first, because it was the first historico-political discourse on society, and it was very different from the philosophico-juridical discourse on society that had been habitually spoken until then. And the historico-political discourse that appeared at this moment was also a discourse on war, which was understood to be a permanent social relationship, the ineradicable basis of all relations and institutions of power." (Foucault 2003 Pg. 49). This discourse arose in contradiction to the hegemonic philosophico-juridical discourse of the time that was constituting monarchical rule then. Both discourses are then engaged in a fight for dominance, they are structured in vastly different and contradictory discursive manners and constitute social orders, mechanisms of power and power/force relations that are very different. The philosophico-juridical discourse utilises the mechanism of law and sovereignty, while the historico-political discourse emphasises the mechanism of power to differentiate between humans and human groups into a binary structure of superiority/inferiority. A state of war exists between groups/races therefore all means by which to win this ongoing never-ending war as long as the inferior exist must be solely afforded to the superior group. This discourse then manufactures the logic of the "Final Solution." This historico-political discourse was formulated to assault the hegemony of philosophico-juridical discourse, therefore its discursive content was in response to that of its enemy discourse. Its worldview was only coherent when viewed in the context of that of its enemy discourse.

As both discourses have evolved over time and are still engaged in a battle for dominance it is not only necessary to trace the evolutionary paths of both discourses, but more importantly the hybrid discourses that have emerged as a result of this longstanding discursive engagement. Foucault states that the first incarnation of the discourse of race war was in England at the beginning of the great political struggles of the seventeenth century, then reappeared in France in the late eighteenth century. Then in the late nineteenth century it appeared as the racist biologists and eugenicists of Europe. There are then two discernible flows in this discursive river: the binary environment between classes, hence class struggle where the contending groups are of the same race and the binary environment between the master race (white) and the inferior races (non-white), hence race war literally. There are two discourses that constitute the mechanisms of power for both binary environments and both have indicated over time the ability to absorb discursive lines from dominant scientific discourse or from the discourse of race war and adapt to operational terrain and spaces where the discourse is not dominant or its dominance is under constant challenge. What also must be understood is the impact of history and the colonial enterprise on the evolution of the discourse of race war in the USA and Canada, and the impact of waves of non-white immigration in Europe in the 20th and 21st centuries on the evolution of the discourse of race war, and its impact on 21st century European politics with the rise of neo-fascism and neo-national socialism. Across the North Atlantic it is then apparent that the discourse of race war interacting with the power relations of conquest and the colonial enterprise has generated a strident discourse of white supremacy, that survives to this day from the seventeenth century, as it has now been absorbed into the discursive matrix of the North Atlantic that constitutes individuals as subjects of power and objects of knowledge. The biopolitics of the West, its mechanisms of power and structures of knowledge contain discursive lines of class/race war, class/race struggle, white supremacy and the policing of race and class binaries as grave threats to the order of power or the militarisation of policing and the criminalisation of protest. This new evolutionary phase is the result of the embrace of the discourse of neoliberalism and its impact on the State and the effectiveness of biopolitics. For neoliberalism insists on an economistic discourse of power with a discourse of politics glaringly congruent with that of the discourse of race war. The cult of neoliberalism driving the politicians of the North Atlantic has then completed the milieu that enables the return of fascism, national socialism and white supremacy to positions of power in the political structures of Europe. From the Brexiteers of both dominant political parties of the UK to Le Pen of France, Wilders of Holland, the AFD and the rest of Germany, Orban of Hungary and those of Austria, Italy and Sweden are all symptoms of this discursive reality.

Binary Concept: Race and Class

Foucault in his genealogy describes the discursive construct of the discourse of race war. Foucault states: "this is the first time the binary conception has been articulated with a specific history. There are two groups, two categories of individuals, or two armies, and they are opposed to each other." (Foucault 2003 Pg. 51). The binary conception which is rooted in history not in a philosophical or juridical context. This grounding history means that the discourse is only concerned with "I" or "We" of the binary groups and the "I" and "We" are defined by, rooted in and made real by history, however mythic. The "I" and the "We" articulates a discourse of personal struggle within the context of the general struggle generated by the binary opposites, not the universalist, totalising or neutral subject constituted by the philosophico-juridical discourse. Foucault states: "Of course, he speaks the discourse of rights, asserts a right and demands a right. But what he is demanding and asserting is his "rights" ...It might be the right of his family or race, the right of superiority or seniority, the right of triumphal invasions, or the right of recent or ancient occupations. In all cases, it is a right that is both grounded in history and decentered from a juridical universality." (Foucault 2003 Pg. 52). The person speaking from the discourse of race war defines rights in a manner that is vastly different and in contradiction to the definition of rights that emanate from the philosophico-juridical discourse. These are rights grounded in the history proclaimed by the discourse and has no concept of juridical universality, hence universal principles that impact a juridical subject are absent and void. Foucault states: "It is interested in the totality only to the extent that it can see it in one sided terms, distort it and see it from its own point of view. The truth is, in other words, a truth that can be deployed from its combat position, from the perspective of the sought for victory and ultimately so to speak, of the survival of the speaking subject himself." (Foucault 2003 pg.52). The discourse of race war cannot see the totality, so there is no totality and the universalizing mechanism that drives it in the discourse of race war. All this discourse can see is the individual and group engaged in battle for dominance with the binary "other" and the strategizing path to victory. A totality, a universal truth are means to victory that you capture, re-tool and unleash towards victory. Adherents of the discourse of race war in the political arena are incapable of visualising the universal maxims as nation, rule of law and rights under law, for there is only the enemy, the constant war with the enemy and the overriding crush for victory by any means necessary as the group and the individual belonging to the group trumps the totality and its totalising principles and its truth. Foucault continues: "It is rather about establishing a right marked by dissymmetry, establishing a truth bound up with a relationship of force, a truth-weapon and a singular right. The subject who is speaking is-I wouldn't even say a polemical subject-a subject who is fighting a war." (Foucault 2003 Pgs.53-54). The speaker from within this discourse is insisting on, demanding and claiming the entitlement of a singular right: the right to truth that belongs only to his discourse. Truth is then linked to force, the threat of the application of force, hence truth is the weapon, the truth-weapon. The enemy "other" defined by this discourse has no singular right to truth, no truth-weapon and no entitlement to claim truth. To challenge the truth of this discourse unleashes the weapon that truth envelops. Welcome to Caribbean colonial domination and the paranoid fear of the domination of the "other" over the master race minority. Or the threat posed by the other/enemy to the USA and Canada. Welcome to the ideal that drives Trump and the neo-fascists and neo-national socialists of Europe. Welcome to western media in the 21st century.

How then does this discourse of race war explain the social order in light of these realities? Foucault states: "This discourse is essentially asking the elliptical god of battles to explain the long days of order, labour, peace, and justice. Fury is being asked to explain calm and order." (Foucault 2003 pg. 54). These are aberrations indicative of weakness of the dominant groups which must be now awakened from their slumber, or removed, giving rise to those who will apply the fury for greatness is only attained via fury. Make America Great Again! Such is one explanation proffered by the discourse. How then does this discourse explain history? Foucault insists that there are principles utilised to explain history as follows: "a series of brute facts, which might be already described as physico-biological facts: physical strength, force, energy, the proliferation of one race, the weakness of another, and so on. A series of accidents, or at least contingencies: defeats, victories, the failure or success of rebellions, the failure or success of conspiracies or alliances, and finally, a bundle of psychological and moral elements (courage, fear, scorn, hatred, forgetfulness, et cetera). Intertwining bodies, passions and accidents according to this discourse, that is what constitutes the permanent web of history and societies." (Foucault 2003 pg. 54). The focus of the discourse of race war is the group and the individual bound to a group, for without the group and the race there is no individual identity. Engaged in a war between binary opposites where history is made by and driven by the characteristics and actions of humans at war. But this is not a war between equals as one race is inherently superior and the opponent is inferior necessitating the position that the race, the group and the individual locked in war drives and manufacture history. All the attributes of human action especially and specifically human action in race war is the material of history and singled out for elite listing. The race war prosecuted by the inherently superior race, the group and especially the individual in a maximum leadership position is the motive force of history. This is the most potent and extreme expression of narcissistic humanism to emerge from the North Atlantic. The humanism of a superior race that can only see itself, gaze upon itself and view the world as its property. The discursive flow that feeds the discourse of white supremacy in the 21st century. A discursive flow that can only constantly visualise incessant war, salient threats and the ever present threat of the race apocalypse must constantly visualise "Final Solutions." In this perceptual and action context history driven by physico-biological "facts" demands the constant generation of mythic historical discourse lashed to discourses of victimhood and past glory. This is potently seen in the discursive flow in Europe in the 21st century in response to the movement of Muslim and Arab refugees from Syria.

Foucault in his genealogy of the discourse of race war presents the power-effect of the discourse as follows: "We have an axis based upon a fundamental and permanent irrationality, a crude and naked irrationality, but which proclaims the truth," "Reason on the side of wild dreams, cunning, and the wicked." "Truth is therefore on the side of unreason and brutality; reason, on the other hand, is on the side of wild dreams and wickedness." (Foucault 2003 pg. 55). Foucault insists that the explanatory axis of the discourse of race war is the binary opposite of the explanatory axis of the discourse of the law and history of the philosophico-juridical discursive flow. The discourse of law and history reduces right and history to an essence of actions and accidents bound up with a discourse of fairness and the good. But what happens when there is a blending of elements of both axes at the local level and at the levels of the political sphere and the oligarchy? What happens when the cult of neoliberalism hinders the operational effectiveness of biopolitics, thereby enabling and facilitating the blending of the binary discourses at the local and macro levels? You have the

North Atlantic in the second decade of the 21st century where white supremacy is now mainstream. On the specific and unique characteristics of the discourse of race war Foucault states: "that it is a discourse that develops completely within the historical dimension. It is deployed within a history that has no boundaries, no end, and no limits." (Foucault 2003 pg. 55). This is a constructed history, a history by its nature is constituted by the discursive flow that enables, operationalises and justifies the power-effects of the discourse. A discourse of barbarity. Foucault continues: "this may well be the first exclusively historico-political discourse-as opposed to a philosophico-juridical discourse to emerge in the West; it is a discourse in which truth functions exclusively as a weapon that is used to win an exclusively partisan victory. It is a sombre, critical discourse, but it is also an intensely mythical discourse; it is a discourse of bitterness...but also of the most insane hopes." (Foucault 2003 Pg. 57). This discourse, the binary opposite of the hegemonic discourse of the North Atlantic must then be banished to the margins, but what are the strategies deployed by the discourse of race war to avoid being marginalised as a subjugated, silenced knowledge and what is the nature of the power relations between both discourses from the 1630's in England when it first appeared to the present? The most powerful tactic adopted by the discourse of race war which has survived the passage of time is the reformulation of the threat posed by non-whites to the white race within a historical context and the propagation of strategies to police and normalise the threat thereof. This discourse absorbed the Socialist concept of class war, turning it into a most potent weapon in its arsenal in its quest for hegemony, where the proletariat in the North Atlantic differentiates itself on the basis of race and undertakes political action driven by race interests. The class war of the discourse in the 21st century is now supplanted by the race/class war ensuring that Marxist socialism and its revisionist pink form social democracy, originally manufactured to serve hegemonic discourse, is now dead in the politics of Europe.

Foucault states that at the end of the sixteenth century and at the beginning of the seventeenth century the discourse of race war was reformulated to mount an assault on, to challenge royal power prominently manifested in England in the 1630's. Foucault states: "The war that is going on beneath order and peace, the war that undermines our society and divides it in a binary mode is, basically, a race war." (Foucault 2003 pgs. 59-60). The discourse in recognition of the hegemony of its binary opposite recognizes that there is order and peace but insists that there is a raging war beneath this order. The discourse of victimhood at the hands of the binary enemy the "other" is formulated and unleashed and the discourse of the imminent threat is joined at the hips with it. Foucault continues: "At a very early stage, we find the basic elements that make the war possible, and then ensure its continuation, pursuit, and development: ethnic differences, differences between languages, different degrees of force, vigour, energy, and violence, the difference between savagery and barbarism; the conquest and subjugation of one race by another." (Foucault 2003 pg. 60). Difference was then the basis for the classification into a binary formulation. Difference that was palpable and historical with the early presence of ethnic differences in the mix, but what of the impact of the West Indian colonial enterprise which included West Africa on the classification of and the constituting of the binary? Was the West Indian colonial enterprise the great laboratory of the discourse of race war out of which emerged the discourse of white supremacy and apartheid as the institutional structure to police and normalise such social orders? Foucault continues: "The social body is basically articulated around two races. It is this idea that this clash between two races runs through society from top to bottom which we see being formulated in the seventeenth century. And it forms the matrix for all the forms beneath which we can find the face and mechanisms of social warfare." (Foucault 2003 pg. 60). The evolution of the definition and classification of the two races is then of seminal importance towards understanding the nature of the discourse in the 21st century and its impact on the North Atlantic today.

Foucault presents the second stage of the evolution of the discourse which was in France at the time of the French Revolution and especially in the early eighteenth century where two distinct streams emerged. One stream was the openly biological transcription which "gives birth to the theory of races in the historico-biological sense of the term." (Foucault 2003 pg. 60). This theory is the first developmental stage in the evolution of the scientific binary discourse of white supremacy/non-white inferiority. In the eighteenth century it articulates two distinct and separate objectives and worldviews: the nationalist struggles of Europe, especially those nationalist struggles against grand State apparatuses as in Russia and Austria; and an articulation of the objectives and worldview of European colonisation where racial superiority now embraces manifest destiny and the white man's burden. This is the first biological transcription of the theory of permanent struggle and race struggle. In this session Foucault devotes very little lecture time to the biological transcription as he is very much interested in the second transcription as it points to the contribution the Socialist project of Karl Marx, especially his discourse of the class struggle, to the evolution of the discourse of race war and its assault on the hegemony of the discourse of law and sovereignty. Foucault states: "And then you find a second transcription based upon the great theme and theory of social war, which emerges in the very first years of the nineteenth century, and which tends to erase every trace of racial conflict in order to define itself as class struggle." (Foucault 2003 pg.60). The discourse by the early nineteenth century has now developed a supposedly binary or bi-polar structure where the historico-biological discourse of race is in contradiction to the discourse of class struggle where all forms of societal struggle, including race war, are subservient to class struggle. All racist discourses are the product of the mode of production and the class struggle that emanates from the mode of production, which means that to resolve racism the mode of production must be changed and the class struggle resolved in favour of the working class. This discourse of the fetish of the working class is publicly locked in battle with white supremacists presently in the North Atlantic, but they share a common discursive origin and flow. This is then a battle for supremacy within the parameters of their common discourse. Foucault's emphasis on the second transcription/class struggle is understandable given the impact of this discourse on the North Atlantic until the collapse of the Soviet Union whilst the colonial enterprise was comparatively remote, but what happens when the products of the colonial and neo-colonial experiments move to Europe in waves without an invitation? The discourse of class struggle and the historico-biological discourse in their power relations reformulate the concept of historico-biological race by taking the initial concept of a race and defining it as a single race with a binary division of superrace and a subrace. Foucault states: "By this I mean the idea-which is absolutely new and which will make the discourse function very differently-that the other race is basically not the other race that came from elsewhere or that was, for a time, triumphant and dominant, but that it is a race that is permanently, ceaselessly infiltrating the social body, or which is, rather, constantly being re-created by the social fabric. In other words, what we see as a polarity, as a binary rift within society, is not a clash between distinct two races. It is the splitting of a single race into superrace and a subrace." "it is the reappearance, within a single race, of the past of that race. In a word, the obverse and the underside of the race reappears within it." (Foucault 2003 pg. 61). Class struggle in its hegemony over the discourse in Europe has reformulated and reformatted the discourse to address European reality in the nineteenth century and thereafter where the binary rift appears within the class/race group with the binary of superrace and a subrace sharing a common biologico-historical legacy. Two questions arise: what is the mechanism of power constituted by this new discursive formulation and what of the evolution of the biologico-historical discourse of the colonial enterprise of the North Atlantic? In the nineteenth century Britain and France abolished slavery in its colonial enterprise as did the USA, this development dramatically impacted the evolution of the strain of the discourse that constituted white supremacy. The new formulation of the discourse has now placed class warfare as the paramount expression of the discourse of race war; where persons of the same genetic lineage are engaged in a grave, fratricidal battle for dominance as they are binary opposites. But this reformulation is flexible as it enables the strain of the discourse focused on biologico-historical race to reformulate itself with the focus on the inevitable war between the superrace (white) and the subrace (non-white). And both strains share a common discourse of power, mechanism of power and apparatuses of power. On this discourse of power Foucault states: "It will become the discourse of centered, centralised and centralising power. It will become the discourse of a battle that has to be waged not between races, but by a race that is portrayed as the one true race, the race that holds power and is entitled to define the norm, and against those who deviate from the norm, against those who pose a threat to the biological heritage." (Foucault 2003 pg. 61). The discourse of power of this reformulation, in other words its new format, injects into the discourse the concept of class and biologico-historical race superiority, class and biologico-historical race power and class and biologico-historical race entitlement. The discourse of white superiority is then the product of this discourse of power, making white supremacy an apparatus of power by which you normalise the social order; whilst the discourse of neoliberalism is an apparatus of power of this discourse by which you put the subrace in their designated place, thereby normalising the social order. Both apparatuses are applied to all spaces in the 21st century social order of the North Atlantic. Foucault continues: "At this point we have all of those biological-racist discourses of degeneracy, but also all those institutions within the social body which makes the discourse of race struggle function as a principle of exclusion and segregation, as a way of normalising society." (Foucault 2003 pg. 61). The reformulated and reformatted discourse constitutes the biological-racist discourses, a stream of which takes on the veneer of being "scientific", whilst at the macro level of the discourse the State institutions are actively engaged in normalising the social order through the application of the apparatuses of exclusion and segregation. Foucault is then indicating that the discourse of race war has an operational presence and existence within the social order dominated by the discourse of biopolitics. Hegemonic power in the North Atlantic has then an operational need for the discourse of race war and its mechanism and apparatuses of power. The banlieues are then the product of the normalising efforts of the discourse of biopolitics. They are wilfully generated, not the product of failed policy, oversight, bad luck and happenstance, for this is where you store your subraces. What then happens when the discourse of biopolitics is weakened to the extent where a grab for dominance by the discourse of race war is inevitably successful? Foucault is insisting that at a specific point in the evolution of the discourse of race war the initial basic formulation was abandoned and replaced by a racist formulation and a thematic that infected the European State which came to fruition in the 20th century, the century of two World Wars that both started in Europe. By the end of the nineteenth century and into the 20th century the discourse of biopolitics was now operationally a hybrid form that developed with the merging of select aspects of the discourse of race war, especially with its mechanism of power. In the post-World War Two era the next era of hybridisation was to add the discourse of neoliberalism, its discourse of power and its mechanism of power to the witches' brew. This has facilitated the grab for dominance by the discourse of race war in the second decade of the 21st century. In all of these evolutionary stages ,commencing with the reformulated and reformatted discourse of race war, the racist thematic is hegemonic in all applications of the discourse, even in social orders where the superrace and the subrace are white, giving rise to State racism where operationally the mechanism of power and the apparatuses of power utilised by the State are racist and driven by the worldview of a racist order. Foucault describes that condition as follows: "At this point, the racist thematic is no longer a moment in the struggle between one social group and another; it will promote the global strategy of global conservatism." Racism as an instrument of normalisation of the individual and the social order drives the social strategy of social conservatism or those opposed to posed threats to the order they prefer. The power to define and police the normative held by the superrace is applied with the instrument of racist policing and suppression. This does not mean that the subrace is above the application of the racist instrument to their quest to exercise power for the racist instrument becomes accepted operational procedure for all of the social order. Foucault states: "we see the appearance of a State racism: a racism that society will direct against itself, against its own elements and its own products. This is the internal racism of permanent purification, and it will become one of the basic dimensions of social normalisation." (Foucault 2003 pg. 62). This State racism is then the cleansing mechanism, the instrument of eugenics that biopolitics cannot envisage or constitute but the need to defend the society, the social order is paramount. To erase this deficiency, the product of the process of hybridisation with the discourse of race war produces the means to permanently purify the social order. You simply institutionalise those deemed mentally and physically unfit leaving them to die in state institutions from abuse and neglect as in 20th century US asylums, you house others in the ghettoes of the urban sprawl and you incarcerate the convicted with lengthy sentences for all crime, non-violent included. But inevitably this instrument of normalisation leads to formulations of the "Final Solution" and "Ethnic Cleansing" for it's a given in the DNA of State racism as a state wages war on its citizens towards cleansing its citizenry of those deemed unfit in the interest of an oligarchy/superrace. What is apparent is the continued application of "internal racism" to the social order with a racist thematic in conjunction with the policing of a class premised hierarchy as they combine to become part of the apparatuses of power charged with normalising the social order. Foucault is insisting that the European development of State racism is an expression of a centered, centralised and centralising power driven by a racist discourse of race war. This centered, centraled and centralising power of the racist European state will then pose the most potent threat to the potency and normalising power of the discourse of western liberal democracies. The discourse that was embraced to serve biopolitics has effectively challenged in the 21st century the traction of the discourse of democracy and individual rights and freedom with the targets of normalisation. This is readily apparent in the rise to power of politicians openly embracing the discourse of State racism in mainstream electoral North Atlantic politics and the swing to this discourse by those seeking electoral politics sustainability in the second decade of the 21st century and thereafter.

Chapter Three
Session Four: 28 January 1976
Race Purity, State Racism

In this session Foucault deals with the genesis of racism and the Nazi and Soviet transformation of race purity and State racism. Foucault states that the historical discourse that appeared in the late sixteenth and early seventeenth centuries was in fact a discourse that was different, even unique in the flow of discourses in Europe. Foucault states: "Historical discourse was no longer the discourse of sovereignty, or even race, but a discourse about races, about a confrontation between races, about the race struggle that goes on within nations and within laws. To that extent it is, I think, a history that is the complete antithesis of the history of sovereignty, as constituted up to that time. This is the first non-Roman or anti-Roman history that the West had ever known." (Foucault 2003 pg. 69). The discourse of race struggle is anathema to the discourse of law and sovereignty and they are locked in a power relation towards exercising hegemony over each other. The discourse of race war discards hegemonic discursive platforms of European civilisation that were absorbed from Roman and Greek civilisations, especially law and sovereignty. The discourse of law and sovereignty is the cement that binds the matrix of the North Atlantic social order into a cohesive, operational, palpable whole. The discourse of race war challenges the very sustainability of this social order and in a genealogy of this discourse it is of extreme importance to articulate the terms of endearment both discourses have worked out since the early seventeenth centuries. The discourse of race war is openly challenging the hegemony of law for it, the hegemony of law, is the expression of the will and right of the powerful over the powerless, whilst the discourse of race war speaks for the powerless, for upon whom the law is exerted in favour of the powerful, those who formulate and police the law made to their benefit. Law is never a universal principle where the rule of law is the universal impartial arbiter for law can only be the instrument of the oppressor. Sovereignty is the expression of the power wielded by the powerful as it is an instrument that binds the powerless to their weakness, their oppression and their oppressor. Power then is the visible living expression of the means, ability and might exercised by the oppressor over the oppressed. Power, law and sovereignty are all expressions of weakness, powerlessness and the life of those enveloped by them. Out of this discourse emerges the concept of repression. The voice of and the speech of this discourse is then driven by the strategic imperative to disrupt, to challenge and to assault the discourse of law and sovereignty, but it does this in an anti-Roman manner, thereby it embraces the instruments of prophecy and promise. For this discourse promises and prophecises signal the rise of an anti-social order, anathema to that of the discourse of law and sovereignty, the two potent examples being the Soviet Union and Nazi Germany. Foucault states: "the appearance of a form of history that is a direct challenge to the history of sovereignty and kings-to Roman history-and that we see a new history that is articulated around the great biblical form of prophecy and promise." (Foucault 2003 pg. 71). In the discourse of race war power is defined in terms of the fact that we are powerless and power is our entitlement by dint of our identity, our history, our lineage and the fact that we are unique as a result. There is no qualitative navel gazing on universal principles of goodness, righteousness and moral fitness to exercise power. Power is an instrument that belongs solely to the elite race, the gifted, the chosen ones and it is their entitlement. They therefore wield power without being encumbered by law and rights. Foucault states: "it is not only a critique of power, but also an attack on it and a demand. Power is unjust not because it has forfeited its noblest examples, but quite simply because it does not belong to us." (Foucault 2003 pg. 73). For Foucault the appearance of the discourse of the race war signalled the end of antiquity in Europe as a brand new, unique historical consciousness emerges focused on an assault on the form and structure of hegemonic power of the era. But the discourse in its evolution shows the tactile ability to develop differing strands of discourse with different strategies in tow making it a polyvalent discourse which is not most of all the voice of the oppressed. It is the voice of those to which power is rightfully due but stolen, denied and under great threat from enemies, the story line for great bloodletting. Foucault states: "This is then, a mobile discourse, a polyvalent discourse. Although its origins lie in the Middle Ages, it is not so marked by them that it can have only one political meaning." (Foucault 2003 pg. 77). The discourse is then polyvalent because it has evolved multiple distinct streams of political meaning during its evolution. Starting with the use of it by various forces opposed to monarchical sovereign power in England, then its use by the aristocrats of France in their opposition to the French sovereign and its use in the colonial enterprise to dominate the colonised subraces. Following this was the development of State racism in Europe and the North Atlantic.

In dealing with the use of "race" in the discourse Foucault speaks of the manner in which "race" is conceptualised and defined for it is a central concept in the discourse from the inception. The word is not pinned to a standard, given meaning as it varies over time and usage, but it is placed in a restricted range which ultimately allows a biological definition that evolves over time. A biological definition that is rooted in a historico-political divide which allows "race" to embrace groups within a given biologically defined "race" such as classes within the white race thereby forming the class/race continuum. There is then the race as a biological entity continuum and the class as a race continuum all existing within a single discursive stream with its accompanying mechanism and apparatuses of power applied to the social order of the 21st century North Atlantic. This historico-political divide then drives the discourse and in the course of the evolution of the discourse the internal power relations of the discourse throw up specific stages of discourse which mark the evolutionary path. Foucault states: "one might say-and this discourse does say- that two races exist whenever one writes the history of two groups which do not, at least to begin with, have the same language or, in many cases the same religion. The two groups form a unity and a single polity only as a result of wars, invasions, victories, and defeats, or in other words acts of violence. The only link between them is the link established by the violence of war." (Foucault 2003 pg. 77). The two groups are differentiated on the basis of identity, culture and worldview where their differences are palpable but not necessarily biological in nature. These two groups share a common space, social order and political structure but this is the product of wars of conquest and the artifice of violence. There is then an underlying tension that is the basis for further violence with both sides being able to utilise the discourse of race war to mount their bid to retain hegemony or to win hegemony, such is the polyvalent nature of the discourse. The colonial enterprise throws together forces that stimulate a strain of this discourse on steroids as the two groups are biologically, culturally and worldview distinct, separate and apart. Which enables the discourse to frame difference and sum it up in terms of biologico-historical references which creates the concept of biological race difference and race supremacy. Foucault continues: "And finally, we can say that two races exist when there are two groups which, although they coexist, have not become mixed because of the differences, dissymmetries, and barriers created by privilege, customs and rights, the distribution of wealth, or the way in which power is exercised." (Foucault 2003 pg.77). Two races exist within a single social order when the differences between both of them are never erased through hybridisation. The race group exercising hegemony has then to police difference as the premier instrument of normalisation in this social order. The policing of normalisation has to preserve difference and ensure the privilege of those wielding power is sustainable. The State has then to constantly formulate and implement structures, institutions and laws that implant privilege/discrimination, access/denial of access, opportunity/denial of opportunity on the landscape of the social order. Whilst the State and the members of the social order forever gaze in expectation of social violence for only violence can bring about change in this order. The apartheid structure of the colonial plantation and then South Africa are then extreme manifestations of this expectation which only the colonial enterprise can generate. But today we see flashes of this expectation in the North Atlantic in the expectation of attacks from Islamic extremists whilst the solutions proffered flow from the colonial plantation/apartheid paradigm. This is then a discourse that has grave problems in formulating a dynamic of organic change for violence is its only dynamic of a nature that must always result in devastation of the social order. The discourse of race war cannot then explain the order and stability of European society in the post second World War era, much less the rise to world hegemonic power of the USA from the end of the Civil War (1865) to the end of the second World War (1945). It cannot explain the North Atlantic social reality where the violence is turned inwards within the subrace rather than towards the superior race in both the class/race and the race continuums. There is then a hegemonic discourse at work in the social order of the North Atlantic which interacts with and holds the discourse of race war in a subservient position, which Foucault terms the discourse of Biopolitics. Foucault in fact in this session mentions the interaction between discourses and the production of knowledges that arise from it as follows: "So the clash between the history of sovereignty and the history of the race war leads to a perpetual interaction, and to the production of fields of knowledge and of knowledge contents." (Foucault 2003 pg. 78). There is then a cross fertilisation between discourses which modifies both discourses and changes the nature of the power relation between both discourses; which has enabled the discourse of race war in the 21st century to especially mount its challenge in the political arena of North Atlantic states.

The Revolutionary Project

Foucault then traces the link between the European concept of revolution and the discourse of race war and its history of insurrection. The Western idea of revolution is then directly linked to the counterhistory of the discourse of race war specifically through its concepts of the terrain and environment that demands warfare, the race/class that must engage in warfare and only the use of social violence will ensure security, power and progress. This counterhistory enabled the creation of the discourse of revolution and the revolutionary project in Europe which in the nineteenth century had evolved to the stage where class struggle had now replaced race war as the core discursive concept. But this was not the only development as the discourse of biological race in this period was under reformulation, which created a discourse of race war focused on the concept of biological race. This evolutionary stage of the nineteenth century will change the discourse fundamentally and exert hegemony within the discourse as never before. What must be noted is the historical precedent for this development as in the sixteenth to seventeenth centuries in the English terrain there was the development of the discourse of race as palpable difference within a god given natural order. In the eighteenth century during the French Revolution there was the development of the discourse of race war with race as being part of the natural order where the white race is entitled to all that accrues from the colonial enterprise. This was in opposition to Jacobin revolutionary, in some cases ultra-revolutionary, discourse visibly expressed in the move to abolish slavery and evolve the colonial enterprise into unacceptable vistas. The discourse of race summed up eloquently by the concept of the colonial enterprise was then in a battle with the revolutionary project. What happens in the nineteenth century when class war replaces race war as the dominant concept of the discourse of race war? Does the revolutionary project now infect the discourse paving the way for the dominance of the concept of race as inalienable difference, hence grave threat and the birth of racism, white supremacy and state racism? Foucault states: "The history of the revolutionary project and revolutionary practise is, I think, indissociable from the counterhistory." "it is indissociable from the appearance from the counterhistory of races and the role played in the West by clashes between races." (Foucault 2003 pg. 79). Foucault's position is in fact addressing multiple realities as the revolutionary project is linked to the counterhistory of race war, races and the impact of clashes between races in Europe. These are the impacts of the clashes with races as white, yet different as the Norse raiders to the English, and there are the clashes with those who are culturally and physically different, as the Mongol hordes and the Muslim raiders. Foucault is then sketching a reality found in the texts of the European revolutionary tradition of the nineteenth century and thereafter in living colour via racist colonial discourse in your face. The European revolutionary project was then infected by the racism of the nineteenth century and thereafter of the counterhistory. Foucault states: "at the time when the notion of race struggle was about to be replaced by that of class struggle" "at the time when this conversion was going on, it was in fact only natural that attempts should be made by one side to recode the old counterhistory not in terms of class, but in terms of races-races in the biological and medical sense of that term." (Foucault 2003 pg.80). The revolutionary project of the nineteenth century was now dominant in the discourse of race war illustrated by the wiping away of the concept of race war and the continued assault on the concept replacing it with class war as the locus of history. This was now a reformulated counterhistory still enthralled with violence as the single, only method of social change so determined by history. One reaction to this rejection of race war was to embrace a reformulated concept of race rooted in the bio-medico discourses of the nineteenth century which was part of the "scientific" structure of the mechanism and apparatuses of power of the day in Europe. The discourse of race war thereafter exhibited two streams within its hegemonic discourse and the mechanism and apparatuses of power. Foucault continues: "another counterhistory began to take shape-but it will be a counterhistory in the sense that it adopts a biologico-medico perspective and crushes the historical dimension that was present in this discourse. You thus see the appearance of what will become actual racism." (Foucault 2003 pg. 80). In response to the revolutionary project to replace race war with class struggle, the discursive response banishes the historical dimension to the discourse of race war replacing it with biologico-medical definitions of race where your race is the threat, not the historical record of race war, giving birth to "actual racism" where your race is a "soul" placed on your body which signals all that you are physically, morally, intellectually, sexually and all that you own and control divorced from and devoid of historical context. The subrace is now a 'thing', an 'it' and most important of all a grave threat that demands purging from the social order. There is then racism that arises from a historical legacy and "actual racism" where you are thingified. But, First Peoples and Africans in the colonial enterprise of the Western hemisphere were stripped of their historical persona and thingified before the nineteenth century under the power relations of the European colonial enterprise in the colonies. What then must be specified is that in nineteenth century Europe the discourse of the 'thingified' races of the colonial enterprise was brought to Europe, reformulated using the biologico-medical scientific discourses of the day, and released with its subsequent impact upon Europe and the North Atlantic. Foucault continues: "the theme of historical war-... will be replaced by the postrevolutionist theme of the struggle for existence." "a struggle in the biological sense: the differentiation of species, natural selection, and the survival of the fittest species." (Foucault 2003 pg. 80). The inferior then presents a grave threat to the peace, order, stability, sustainability and the genetic purity of the superior race, an existential threat. Driven by this construct the discourse discards the concept of the binary society replacing it with the society that is biologically monist. This results in the identification of, and policing of, heterogeneity and difference, where the grave threats to the monist social order are posed by deviants spawned by difference and heterogeneous groups in the social order and the infiltration of foreigners into the social order breeding heterogeneity and difference. This is the discourse of paranoid policing towards normalisation not afraid to medicalise difference, summed up in the scientific discourse of the abnormal. What is then clearly apparent is that "actual racism" appears where the antihistorical biologico-medico discourse of race enters the panoply of "scientific" discourse serving hegemonic discourse in the generation of knowledges to serve power, expressed as the power/knowledge nexus. Actual racism is then an organic functionary of the "scientific apparatus" of European hegemonic discourse since the nineteenth century. It is part of the mechanism and apparatuses of power of hegemonic discourse charged with normalising the social order. Racist oppression is then organic to the west, not an aberration, a left over from the colonial enterprise operationalised at local levels. The final concept to complete the architecture of this reformulated "scientific" discourse of actual racism is the dramatically changed conceptualisation of the State.

Racism, the State and State Racism

In the discourse of race war, the State in the hands of the enemy race is an instrument of oppression for that is the purpose of the state. In the discourse of "actual" racism, the State has a biological function for it's the immune system of the master race. Foucault states: "the State is, and must be the protector of the integrity, the superiority and the purity of the race. The ideal of racial purity, with all its monistic, Statist, and biological implications: that is what replaces the idea of race struggle." (Foucault 2003 pg.81). The State is charged with policing the threats posed by the deviants and the foreigners, making the State the premier agent of normalisation. There is then no space in the social order that is shielded from the gaze of the State. Foucault then presents his position on what constitutes racism as follows: "I think that racism is born at the point where the theme of racial purity replaces that of class struggle, and when counterhistory begins to be converted into a biological racism." (Foucault 2003 pg. 81). This position is in itself highly problematic as Foucault is insisting that race hate is only racism when its biologically driven. Foucault does not state how he conceptualises the race hate of the colonial enterprise of the western hemisphere from 1492 until the nineteenth century. Foucault is speaking in a deliberately constructed context in which the genealogy of the discourse of race struggle refers to the colonial enterprise in passing, but there is never any recognition of the impact on the discourse of race hate of the colonial enterprise and its impact on the evolution of discourse in Europe. The role of the planters of the British West Indies, resident in England, in the promulgation of discourse in support of the colonial enterprise and African slavery is the most potent example of the impact of the colonial enterprise on European discourse. Then there is the impact of the East India Company on the evolution of racist discourse in England. Foucault's construct has then to be drastically changed in reference to Europe as it's a much more complex discursive flow and environment. Much more importantly his construct is blind, deaf and dumb when applied to the western hemisphere. In fact, the complexity of the evolution of discourses of race hate to white supremacy in the USA is outside the perceptual mechanism of Foucault's construct. Foucault then presents his justification for his position on racism by stating that racism in Europe only appeared when the discourse of sovereignty captured the discourse of race struggle, using the aperture afforded by the discourse to formulate the discourse of race purity policed, protected and ensured by the State. The discourse of sovereignty did this in order to breathe new life and relevance into the State, ensuring its central role in the social order. Foucault states: "Racism is, quite literally, revolutionary discourse in an inverted form." Foucault 2003 pg. 81). The product of absorbing the revolutionary discourse and redefining its original discourse. But in this position Foucault has to insist that before this act of inversion racism did not exist, for racism is only racism when it's part of the structure of scientific discourse serving hegemonic discourse. But what then existed before scientific discourse appeared? Is this another instance of European denial of the operational reality of the colonial enterprise? Foucault continues: "the discourse of race (in the singular) was a way of turning that weapon against those who had forged it, of using it to preserve the sovereignty of the State, a sovereignty whose lustre and vigour were no longer guaranteed by magico-juridical rituals, but by medico-normalising techniques." (Foucault 2003 pg. 81). The discourse of race war was presenting a revolutionary challenge to hegemonic discourse, especially sovereignty and the State, that was effective necessitating that the discourse of race war be absorbed and reformulated to avert the threat by breathing new life into the discourse of sovereignty. Racism was the instrument devised to defeat the potent bid for dominance mounted by the discourse of race war and to reinvigorate the State by creating a new discursive base for its hegemony: the normalising instrument of scientific medical discourse, which then medicalised threats to the State. Foucault continues: "Thanks to the shift from law to norm, from races in the plural to race in the singular, from the emancipatory project to a concern with purity, sovereignty was able to invest or take over the discourse of race struggle and reutilise it for its own strategy." (Foucault 2003 pg. 81). In the process of the hostile takeover of the discourse of race war the discourse of sovereignty became a discourse possessing streams in conflict within the discourse, a schizophrenic or at best a bipolar discourse; as law and norm, race, purity, rule of law and human rights. The State and hegemonic discourse in this context gives life and operational space to white hegemony as it's an organic expression of the discourse of sovereignty. Was white racism before this event excluded from hegemonic discourse in Europe? No! The only possible difference is the appearance of State racism in Europe, where the State is the guarantor of the race mechanism and the apparatuses of power utilised to ensure order and peace. Foucault states: "State sovereignty thus becomes the imperative to protect the race. It becomes both an alternative to and a way of blocking the call for revolution that derived from the old discourse of struggles, interpretations, demands, and promises." (Foucault 2003 pgs. 81-82). Continued sovereignty became attached to the task of protecting the white race, for this task gave it legitimacy, traction and sustainability in the social order. To do this the social order was then open to and already exposed to a discourse of white supremacy, but not to a discourse of white State racism. Foucault should have then distinguished clearly between State racism and racism, for in his genealogy they are quite dissimilar. In order to blunt the threat of the revolutionary discourse of class struggle, the hegemonic discourse of the nineteenth century created the discourse of a State that was now defined by its commitment to the hegemony of a race and to do all in its power to protect and project the interests of that race. White supremacy was now no longer mounting an assault on the State as it now possessed a State to call its own, thereby ending its revolutionary vigour and ardour which was forfeited by the State. But how did this State racism formed at the end of the nineteenth century in Europe evolve in the twentieth century and what is its legacy it has bequeathed to the world? Foucault states: "At the end of the nineteenth century, we see the appearance of what might be called a State racism, of a biological and centralised racism. And it was this theme, if not profoundly modified, at least transformed and utilised in strategies specific to the twentieth century." (Foucault 2003 pg. 82).

State Racism, Nazi Germany and the Soviet Union

Foucault cites two transformations of State racism in the 20th century that stand above the rest in Europe: Nazi Germany and the Soviet Union. Nazi Germany was the product of the discursive marriage of hegemonic State discourse with elements of the discourse of race struggle before its capture by the discourses of class struggle and sovereignty. State racism was grafted onto the mythic legends of the Aryan Germanic master race attacked, brutalised and ravaged by inferior races intent on preventing the master race from attaining its rightful position as the Lord and Master of Europe and the World. The National Socialist Party under the visionary leadership of Adolf Hitler will destroy all enemies within and without, restoring the Aryan Germanic race to its glorious destiny expressed as the Third Reich. The enemies within the Jews, Roma, Africans, Slavs, physically and mentally challenged and purveyors of opposing discourses must be purged for the strengthening of the Reich. All individuals belonged to the State and the State was the domain of the National Socialist party, making State and party a single operational entity. In fact, national socialist discourse evolved State racism to an existential reality experienced only in the European colonial enterprise, as for example in the Belgian Congo. It implemented colonial apartheid in Europe and took the quest for safety and security from the threat posed by the inferior races to its logical end: The Final Solution. The discourse of the apocalypse of the Germanic master race bound to the discourse of Germanic master race glory and conquest resonated with the German population; illustrated by fits of ecstasy as Hitler addressed his public rallies. This demonstrated the salient reality that the German population was ready and waiting for national socialist discourse by dint of the racist discourses that were long part of European history emanating from the colonial enterprise. Foucault states: "We have then a Nazi reinscription or reinsertion of State racism in the legend of warring races." (Foucault 2003 pg. 82). But, the legend of the Germanic race at war is itself a racist discourse predating the Nazi makeover, again raising the issue of the failure to trace the evolution of the racist colonial discourse that developed in France, for example in response to the revolutionary discourse of the French Revolution, in Foucault's genealogy.

Foucault's Soviet transformation is the binary "other" of the Nazi transformation, as it involved the evolution of a "scientific" discourse of revolutionary class struggle faced with the task of exercising power in a social order engaged with the grave threats of the internal forces of counterrevolution and the external threat of invasion by capitalist imperialist forces external of the Soviet Union. In a social order dominated by the dictatorship of the proletariat, operationalised through the dictatorship of the Communist Party of the Soviet Union, internal counter revolutionary forces must be mentally unsound to reject the fruition of history in favour of the working class. These persons then occupy a space created by the discourse of class struggle, a space of fluid definition, that changes with time as the power relations dictate. These persons are then class enemies, counter revolutionaries, criminals, mentally defective or all of the above, and the social order must be protected at all costs from this dangerous threat to its peace and stability. They are placed in gulags, prison camps, maximum security prisons and asylums, excised from the social order under quarantine. Western capitalist liberal notions of human rights do not enter into this power relation as they are the class enemies of the socialist state. In the post Stalin era in their quest to create a world class "scientific" academy to match and surpass that of the west, the medicalisation of class enemies became one of a range of choices other than the prison regime with the development of dialectical materialist "science." There is then no marriage of legends of the great Slav master race, their past glory and the return to glory under Soviet communism. There is the glory of the workers and peasants of the Soviet Union exercising power over their class enemies and building the Soviet socialist state towards communism. The heroes of the Soviet socialist state are not mythic for they are the workers, the peasants and the leaders of the communist party. This will exponentially explode in depth and grandeur with the invasion of Nazi Germany and victory over the Nazi invaders, which affirmed the accuracy of dialectical materialism and the superiority of the Soviet socialist state under the leadership and hegemony of the communist party. This was then a state under the hegemony of a political form utilising the state as an apparatus of power. The driving conviction of Hitler that the Soviet Union must be destroyed by Nazi Germany for the grave threat it posed to the security of Nazi Germany is then apparent. Revolutionary Soviet communism presented a viable alternative to National Socialist discourse, made especially potent by their footing in a common discourse. Foucault states: "In Soviet state racism, what revolutionary discourse designated as the class enemy becomes a sort of biological threat."

"the weapon that was once used in the struggle against the class enemy... is now wielded by a medical police which eliminates class enemies as though they were racial enemies." (Foucault 2003 pg. 83). In summing up both states Foucault insists that, in spite of the different discourses with different mechanisms and apparatuses of power utilised, they both embraced State racism as the operational mechanism of power relations of the State and social order with its prime concern of keeping the social order pure. Foucault ends this session by stating that the discourse of race war forced on the agenda of Europe a conceptualisation of power where: "the question of power can no longer be dissociated from servitude, liberation, and emancipation." (Foucault 2003 pg. 83). The discourse of race war posed an alternate question of power that was excluded from the question of power posed by hegemonic discourse of sovereignty and law; thereby expressing the condition of engagement between discourses in a quest for dominance. In this engagement there must be discursive agents on both sides of the divide formulating and re-formulating discursive constructs to drive the quest for hegemony. In session five, Foucault will devote his attention to the appearance of the discourse of race in seventeenth century England and the role of the discursive agent of hegemonic discourse Thomas Hobbes. Foucault in this session commences his genealogy of the discourse of specific discursive agents towards presenting the range and complexity of ideas that flowed in the terrain of discursive engagement, thereby illustrating the tactical polyvalence of discourse in its exercise of power.

A deconstruction of the discourse of West Indian slavery as articulated by slave owners/planters and officials of the colonial State resident in the colonies is necessary to interrogate Foucault's distinction between racism and "actual" racism. This study will select published journals from British and French West Indian slave colonies and apply the methodology of deconstruction to unearth the discursive constructs of the discourse of slavery unearthed, which will interrogate Foucault's position.

Chapter Four
Session Five: 4 February 1976

Foucault devotes this session to his genealogy of the discourse of race war in England in the seventeenth century. Foucault states: "In other words, the divide, the perception of the war between races predates the notion of the social struggles or class struggle, but it certainly cannot be identified with a racism of, if you like, the religious type." (Foucault 2003 pg. 88). The discourse of race war in seventeenth century England is vastly different in its composition from its later evolutionary forms. It is devoid of a concept of social struggle which inhibits the development of the concept of class struggle and the concept of race does not lend itself to the development of racism, even of the religious type. What is certain for Foucault is the fact that the discourse stressed on difference as difference was the basis for the "race" war and the necessity of it. Difference and the necessity of war then brought into existence the alternate question on power. This is clearly apparent in the discourse of war given the diametrically opposite position articulated by the discourse of Thomas Hobbes. Foucault states: "You know that this is not at all the case in Hobbes. The primitive war, the war of every man against every man, is born of equality and takes place in the element of that equality. War is the immediate effect of nondifferences, or at least of insufficient differences." (Foucault 2003 pg. 90). Hobbes is insisting that war is the product of insufficient differences where the society is homogenised to the extent where difference and diversity are banished, thereby precipitating wars. For Hobbes then there is a mechanism, a centralised and centralising power that homogenises the mass of people thereby producing a society. Is this the Leviathan? Foucault states: "Hobbes in fact says that if there were great differences, if there really were obvious visible disparities between men, it is quite obvious that war will immediately come to an end. (Foucault 2003 pg. 90). For Hobbes the centralised great centralising power had eliminated difference and disparities, thereby promoting the need for war between men in the domain of this power. Hobbes was clearly and obviously mounting a discursive challenge to the discourse of race war in seventeenth century England. Hobbes was crafting knowledge in the service of power in response to the challenge. Simply a talking head. Hobbes is insisting that there are no differences, hence war is not the given with difference, there is peace as the instrument to blunt the assault, the assault of the discourse of race war. But what is the nature of this state of war of Hobbes given the existence of this centralised and centralising power that has eliminated difference? Foucault states: "The absence of natural differences therefore creates uncertainties, risks, hazards, and therefore the will to fight on both sides; it is the aleatory element in the primal relationship of force that creates the state of war." (Foucault 2003 pg. 91). But, what is this state of war of Hobbes in light of the centralised, centralising and normalising power that erases difference? For this power must have neutralised the state of war as it erases difference to ensure peace and order, provided that the state of war is in fact what the words convey. Foucault states: "that the state Hobbes is describing is not at all a brutish state of nature in which forces clash directly with one another." "There are no battles in Hobbes's primitive war." "We are in a theatre where presentations are exchanged," (Foucault 2003 pg. 92). Difference is then the key for preventing a state of war that is not war, it is a theatrical performance where presentations are exchanged between those in the state of war. Hobbes has then to dismiss the very contention of the discourse of race war. Foucault states: "What does characterise the state of war is a sort of unending diplomacy between rivals who are naturally equal. We are not at war; we are in what Hobbes specifically calls a state of war." (Foucault 2003 pg. 92). In the banishing of difference there are no inequalities, which results in rivals of equal potency and power facing off which demands the state of unceasing diplomacy or the state of war not being at war.

Foucault poses the question of how does a state of war give birth to the State, to Leviathan and to sovereignty? A most intriguing question given the nature of Hobbes's discourse of a state of war. Hobbes posited that there were two categories of sovereignty: by institutions and by acquisition which gave rise to two state forms: states by institutions and by acquisition. Sovereignty by acquisition arises through conquest, through war not a state of war. Sovereignty of acquisition arises from the fear, not of defeat, but the fear of purges and extermination at the hand of the victors at the point of the duality of victory/ defeat. The fear of losing one's life results in the surrender of the defeated to the wishes of the new sovereign. In Hobbes's scenario there is a return to sovereignty that is valid even though it's driven by fear, unlike his other archetype sovereignty by institutions. Foucault states: "The will to prefer life to death: that is what founds sovereignty, and it is as juridical and legitimate as the sovereignty that was established through the mode of institution and mutual agreement." (Foucault 2003 pg. 95). But conquest poses a grave threat to the structure of Hobbes's discourse as it negates the Leviathan of the sovereignty of institutions by dint of war waged and won on the Leviathan. And the potency of this threat is the product of Hobbes's definition of sovereignty, all sovereignty. Foucault states: "For sovereignty to exist, there must be-and this is all there must be-a certain radical will that makes us want to live, even though we cannot do so unless the other is willing to let us live." (Foucault 2003 pg. 96). The threat to life must be real and it must be bolstered by the will to live at all costs, but this will to live at all costs is powerless to attain the end at hand to save one's life. Sovereignty is then premised on the duality of power/powerlessness which drives fear, the fixation with living by any means necessary and the powerlessness of, in spite of all these, one is unable to save one's life. The series is then will, fear and sovereignty. Sovereignty is then the power to generate fear, to engender the fixation with living and most importantly the act of repeated surrender to the powered, in Hobbes's case the sovereign, the Leviathan. In this entire discursive terrain of Hobbes, the gravest threat he recognises to the order of the Leviathan is defeat by conquest where the entire order rooted in the sovereignty of the Leviathan will be extinguished and a new order constructed on its ashes. How does this position apply to the English colonial enterprise that was ongoing in the lifetime of Hobbes? In reality the peoples of the invaded lands were the conquered with their civilisations destroyed and a new order of the conquest created on the ashes. How did these colonial realities return to England as lessons to be learnt and applied to England and Europe?

Hobbes is insisting that conquest in the English context establishes the need to erase difference through the homogenisation of the population. This homogenisation establishes the power relation that is the foundation of sovereignty where fear of death at the hands of the conqueror spawns will to live and the willingness to surrender sustainably, which is the basis of the exercise of sovereignty. Fear, will to live and surrender engaged in a power relationship with the will of sovereignty to grant life is the basis of the state of war. The state of war cannot be war because there is a single conqueror exercising the power of life and death over the defeated/conquered. The grave threat of a conqueror then throws the Hobbesian landscape into chaos and is in fact the only valid reboot possibility of the Hobbesian artifice. In response to the perennial question of Max Weber: Why do men obey? Hobbes posits that obedience is the result of fear of the power over life by a central power and the will to live at all costs. Obedience is then purchased by the exercise of sovereignty, exemplified by potently and expressively taking human life. The peace brought by difference is illusory, for sovereignty and the quest for sovereignty must always drive homogenisation and normalisation; and all forms of conquest demand the operationalisation of sovereignty.

Hobbes is writing to avert another threat of conquest by formulating and releasing his discourse of contracts and sovereignty, which is his discourse of the State. Foucault states: "After all, philosophy and right or philosophico-juridical discourse, would rather give the State too much power than not enough power, and while they do criticise Hobbes for giving the State too much power, they are secretly grateful to him for having warded off a certain insidious and barbarous enemy." (Foucault 2003 pgs. 98-99). What is this grave threat? Foucault continues: "It is this discourse of struggle and permanent civil war Hobbes wards off by making all wars and conquests depend upon a contract, and by thus rescuing the theory of the State." "Hobbes devotes whole sections of Leviathan to attacking a discourse (or rather a practice) which seems to me have appeared-...in England." (Foucault 2003 pg. 99). Hobbes's discourse is formulated to assault the discourse of race war and in this assault he sounded the clarion call to hegemonic discourse to join the assault. Foucault traces the existence of the discourse of conquest and its impact on the formation of the discourse of race war in England in the seventeenth century. From the Norman Conquest of William from 1066 of England all English kings up to Henry VII claimed their power to exercise their sovereignty by right of conquest. There are the series of rebellions in resistance to the Norman conqueror and conquest that were defined as a rebellion against a foreign conqueror and domination by foreigners. This gave rise to the conceptualisation of the Norman/Saxon binary expressed in terms of two races locked in battle for dominance. At the end of the sixteenth century and the beginning of the seventeenth century the battle for dominance between three entities of the social order: the monarchy, the aristocracy and the bourgeoisie, simply created the demand for a discourse to counter hegemonic discourse. With this demand discursive agents simply appropriated the race binary of the conquest, reformulated and released the discourse of race war. Strands of a common discourse of race war were used by all parties in the engagement. Foucault states: "the theory of races did not function as a particular thesis about one group versus another. The racial divide and the systematic opposition between races were in fact a sort of instrument, both discursive and political, that allowed both sides to formulate their own theses." "And so you will find the theory of races, or the theme of races, in the positions of both royal absolutism and the parliamentarians or parliamentarists, and in the more extreme positions of the Levellers and the Diggers." (Foucault 2003 pgs. 101-102). The gravity and intensity of the engagement for hegemony ensured that the extremist wing, the purveyors of absolute monarchism and the aristocrats all formulated a stream of the discourse to serve their strategic ends. But the discourse of conquest was never extinguished in this war between streams and factions of the very same discourse. Foucault's genealogy posits that the discourse of the King comprising conquest and domination is traced all the way back to the Norman conquest of England as expressed by James I of England and Scotland in the seventeenth century. But in sixteenth century England there was then a new twist to the discourse of the King where conquest and domination was the right of the King over the colonies of America and the West Indies, where the Norman conquest and domination of England was the basis of the right of the King to conquer and dominate lands external of England the colonies by right of colonisation. The discourse of the King was then eventually replaced by the discourse of race, then white supremacy. Foucault states: "At the end of the sixteenth century we have then, if not the first, then an early example of the sort of boomerang effect colonial practice can have on the juridico-political structures of the West." (Foucault 2003 pg. 103). Foucault is saying that the discourse, mechanism and apparatuses of colonial power flows back to the metropole and impacts their hegemonic discourse, and its mechanism and apparatuses of power. The nature of colonial power was not static as it evolved to deal with social realities, for example in the British West Indies the discourse of colonial power before the emancipation of the enslaved was markedly different thereafter. What is basic to British colonial discourse is a racist differentiation of the white from the non-white races, of the colonial dominator from the dominated which meant that space in the colony is divided in a binary form, an apartheid system. The binary division of space housed the binary division of the races and there was a blatantly visible hierarchy of spaces occupied by specific races and mixtures with white DNA thereof. The space you occupied was a race space and opportunities available were defined by the race space. How then does this specific order of social control impact the order of the metropole is the question? Foucault states: "it also had a considerable boomerang effect on the mechanisms of power in the West, and on the apparatuses, institutions and techniques of power." (Foucault 2003 pg. 103). Colonial discourse then impacted the nature of power in the metropole, but what was the effect and to what end? Foucault continues: "A whole series of colonial models was brought back to the West, and the result was that the West could practice something resembling colonisation, or an internal colonisation on itself." (Foucault 2003 pg. 103). What constituted this internal colonialism Foucault does not say? What is apparent is that the entry of non-white foreigners into the metropoles as a result of the imperial project led to the colonial model of race space being applied to the social order of Europe where specific segments of space, physical with its own structure, organisation and architecture, policing and ideational order were allocated to non-white race minorities, which in most cases were placed in the deep bowels of space already allocated to the white underclass, the original outcast race nation. Today these spaces are called the banlieues in France, in the USA the inner city/ghetto as the pattern persists well into the 21st century. In the colonial order the race space and its inmates were policed in order to ensure its preservation and the docility of its inmates. Policing of these race spaces was rooted in a process of normalisation, where the cultural patterns of the inmates of the race space were policed and abnormalised in an attempt to saturate the space with policing and to normalise behaviour by prescribing norms to the inmates of the race space. The fundamental basis of the race space was the binary of the races: white and non-white. To transpose this rubric to Europe and impose it on a more or less white population is difficult at best, save and except you replace the race binary with the class binary and label spaces class spaces. But, as the non-white empire derived population builds and begins to dominate specific class spaces the need for the race binary and the race space, even a race/class space, with its attendant apparatuses of power and normalisation becomes pressing. In the USA the First Peoples, the Africans and Hispanics were and are all recipients of the race spaces with its attendant apparatuses of policing and normalisation and other products of the race binary.

The discourse of the parliamentarians comprised the racial dualism and Norman conquest denial. This discourse insisted that William was a rightful heir in line for the throne, hence he did not acquire the throne of England by conquest. Having acquired the throne by rightful inheritance the discourse of conquest is nullified and what in fact exists is a rightful king whose absolute power is circumscribed and limited by existing Saxon law at the time of his coronation. The monarchists and their aristocrat allies are then usurpers by denying the existence and operation of Saxon law which renders the claim of absolute power of the king by right of conquest a lie. Therein lies the binary for the race war. The parliamentarians were then articulating a utopia of Saxon rights which expanded into an early articulation of a discourse of natural rights held by Saxons within the ambit of a political model driven by the dream of the kingdom of God on earth, which in the course of the war evolved into the republic of God on earth. This parliamentarian discourse of the kingdom of God on earth was driven by a conception of political historicism which gave the movement depth, history, meaning and mission with its accompanying legendary conceptions of models of action. The extremist arm of the binary divide rejected the other two sides of the divide making the binary form Levellers and Diggers/monarchists and parliamentarians. The minority Levellers and Diggers, in their rejection of the monarchist and parliamentarian positions, would formulate discursive positions rooted in political historicism that envisaged total revolution making them one of the early discursive expressions of what would come to be known as Marxism and Anarchism in later years. The Levellers insisted that the conquest was fact and that the law established since the conquest serves the monarchists and the aristocrats against those excluded. Law since the conquest was the instrument of oppression and has to be extinguished along with all the differences, inequalities and oppression it legislates. England since the conquest is not the land of absolute right but of tricks, traps and wickedness. The basis of the oppression is the difference the law legislates between aristocrats and the others, difference predicated not on protection of the others, but plunder and theft by the aristocrats. Difference legislated by law is then the basis of difference and oppression. To end oppression difference must be abolished by destroying the law in its entirety. The Diggers adopted a much more revolutionary position by insisting that the permanent war of the conquest never ceased as the post conquest government, laws and property relations are the obverse of war. The permanent war, invasion and defeat of conquest is relived every instance of existence through government, laws and property relations. Which result in the permanent state of rebellion of the people for rebellion is the response to the state of war being waged by the government on the people. The Diggers, as the Levellers, insist that the law of the oppressors must be dismantled. This discourse that was released in England in the seventeenth century redefines the nature of the social order and posits a new method for the study of law, sovereignty and power in the social order. Law, sovereignty and power have to be studied, not in terms of natural rights and the establishment of sovereignty: "but in terms of the unending movement-which has no historical end-of the shifting relations that make some dominant over others." (Foucault 2003 pg. 109). The discourse of race is then openly challenging the hegemony of the discourse of law and sovereignty to its very core worldview. It is insisting that natural rights and the edifice of sovereignty mask deliberately the oppression of the excluded, the different under law, sovereignty and power and must be discarded as there can be no revolutionary project utilising this methodology. What has to be the new method is the never ending history of the dynamic relations that enable a group to dominate, to exercise dominion over another. This then is a method rooted in history and political action which creates a political historicism that is unique in Europe for this epoch. Foucault states: "we see here a binary schema, a certain binary scheme; and for the first time, it functions in both a political and a historical mode, both as a program for political action and a historical mode." (Foucault 2003 pg.109). This discourse invented political historicism as a tool of analysis which placed it in a battle for hegemony with the discourse of law and sovereignty and the discourse of dialectical materialism. But this political historicism also prepared the discursive pathway for the appearance and development of the discourse of racism. Foucault states: "This was the first time that the binary schema that divided society into two races was articulated with national phenomena such as language, country of origin, ancestral customs, the density of a common past, the existence of an archaic right, and the rediscovery of old laws." (Foucault 2003 pg. 110). This unique binary schema of seventeenth century England was the foundation for the formulation of racist colonial discourse, where the rights of conquest were a major rationale utilised for the slave trading and owning colonial enterprise. The rights of conquest merged with the race superiority of the English and the inherent inferiority of the dominated/enslaved drove this discourse, and thus the impact of the colonial enterprise, its history and politics on the evolution of the discourse of race war in England in the seventeenth century must be accepted.

The binary scheme shackled to political historicism presents race war as the primary dynamic of the social order. A dynamic that now posits rebellion as generic to a social order where race war is the basis of the social order. Foucault states: "The justification for rebellion now becomes a sort of historical necessity, it is a response to a certain social order. The social order is a war, and rebellion is the last episode that will put an end to it." (Foucault 2003 pg. 110). The race war constantly begets rebellion, for not all rebellion will be successful, but what is a certainty is the eventual arrival of the apocalyptic battle that ends the race war. In the series of unsuccessful rebellions and the certainty of the final battle this social order is then ultimately unstable. Foucault states: "War is both the web and the secret of institutions and systems of power." (Foucault 2003 pg. 110). Nowhere is this discourse lived as vividly as on the slave plantations of the West Indies and in the colonies, where a minority white race was faced with the imperative to exercise power over an overwhelmingly visible non-white population. The colonial enterprise expressed the extreme form of the social order of the discourse of race war branded on the bodies of the dominated. For Foucault, the political historicism developed by this discourse posed a grave challenge to hegemonic discourse from its emergence in seventeenth century England which demanded relentless engagement towards silencing this discourse thereafter. The driving reason for this is the discursive flow that emanates from political historicism. The foremost concept of the discursive flow was the interpretation of power relations as a state of domination, where the only effective path to liberation was repeated and continuous rebellion until the forces of the power relations of domination are overthrown. Every single institution and discourse of the hegemonic order was therefore challenged in a constant state of war as a politico-historical necessity until liberation is achieved. In the context of England in the seventeenth century, this discourse set in train the movement for the emasculation of the absolute monarchy and the rise of, and eventual hegemony of, secular humanism. Foucault states: "In the longer term, what had to be eliminated was what I would call 'political historicism.'" (Foucault 2003 pg. 111). "we are talking about domination, about an infinitely dense multiple domination that never comes to an end. There is no escape from domination, and there is therefore no escape from history." (Foucault 2003 pg. 111). The specific focus on domination of the discourse of race war dramatically changes the conversation as it cannot include issues of rights and law: public or other forms, as the discourse of race war insists that domination is an absolute, it is history, it is then hegemonic in the history of man and must be embraced as the sustainable normal. This is why the discourse must exclude as it cannot include sovereignty and law, for it must only envisage fear and embrace and extol domination. The rebellion against domination then applies to rights, law and sovereignty and since domination is historical the discourse of race war then faced two potent opponents formulated in response: in the seventeenth century it was the extreme formulations of the philosophico-juridical discourse, of Thomas Hobbes especially, and in the nineteenth century it was dialectical materialism. Dialectical materialism posed its challenge with the concepts of class struggle and the state of communism, where domination will cease to exist; for all domination stems from the nature of ownership of the mode of production, which throws up the class structure and class struggle. With the socialist revolution the changed nature of the ownership of production, combined with the dictatorship of the proletariat, the objective conditions for class struggle are abolished and with it, domination of man by man. This is an approach to power and domination intimately opposed to political historicism and the threat it poses to the quest for hegemony of dialectical materialist discourse.

The basis of Foucault's genealogy is the reawakening of historical knowledges and discourses and his choice of the discourse of race war as the topic of the 1976 public lecture indicates his position on the veracity of this discourse as an able challenger to hegemonic discourse. The genealogy of this discourse presented in 1976 will then illustrate the dynamic of the power relations of Europe from the seventeenth century to the twentieth century.

Chapter Five

Session Six: 11 February 1976, Session Seven: 18 February 1976, Session Eight: 25 February 1976

In sessions six, seven and eight Foucault continues with the presentation of his genealogy of the discourse of race war by turning his view to France, by specifically concentrating on the ideas of specific discursive agents. In keeping with my deconstruction of Foucault's genealogy I am seeking out the salient concepts of Foucault's discourse of relevance to my project.

Session Six

France, Public Right and Germanic Invasion

Foucault insists that in the period preceding the appearance of the discourse of political historicism in France there were no expressions at the time of the Wars of Religion of the idea of duality of any form in the social order. There was discussion of the impact of invasion on the power of the king, public right and the absolute monarch. The discourse of the impact of invasion and conquest on public right involved a debate over the origin of France in a specific epoch identified with a specific ethnic group. The line flowed through the legend of the Franks being the creator of France, liberating what was designated as France from Roman occupation. Then the line evolved to state that the Franks were Germanic invaders removing the Romans and in turn dominating the Gauls. Followed by the line that the Germans were in fact not invaders but brothers of the Gauls as the Roman Imperium was the only invader. The Gauls had relentlessly resisted Roman imperialism and saw the Romans as the enemy, not the German enemy of the Romans. Finally, the line emerges of what Foucault terms "Gallo-centrism", which I term the discourse of the Gallic master race, where the Gauls in fact were the core, the nucleus of all the ethnic groups in Europe, including the Romans. They all came from Gauls who migrated and colonised various parts of Europe from Gaul. In the debate over invasion, conquest and public right in France, the discursive basis of the master race was formulated into existence. This discourse of the Gaul master race was formulated in reaction to the position that France was the product of an invasion and defeat of the Roman imperium over Gaul by Germanic invaders in seventeenth century France. Foucault states: "More important still was the foundation and introduction of an absolutely new thesis, which was to be of fundamental importance. This is the theme of what I would call radical 'Gallo-centrism.'" "But from the seventeenth century onward these Gauls, became the principle or, so to speak, the motor of history." "the Gauls became the first or fundamental element, and the Germans came to be described as a mere extension of the Gauls." (Foucault 2003 pg.122). The German ethnic group that challenged and destroyed the Roman Imperium over Gaul was in fact of Gallic origin as the Gallic ethnic group is the source of the German ethnic group. How? Foucault states: "This was the beginning of a sort of expansion and colonisation, and the French nation became the womb of all the other peoples of Europe (and even peoples outside Europe." (Foucault 2003 pg. 122). In the era of the colonial enterprise sweeping Europe, with the drive to break the Spanish monopoly of the western hemisphere, the French have now formulated a discourse that establishes the foundation for a specific colonial imperial discourse of the French master race in the western hemisphere and by extension the world.

France: Nations, Race, Class and Nationalism

For Foucault the evolutionary change in discursive engagement with hegemonic discourse in France appeared in the late seventeenth century with the battle between sections of the nobility and the absolute monarchy. This was battle, first against hegemonic juridical knowledge in the late seventeenth and early eighteenth centuries, then followed by the intense engagement with economic knowledge in the mid-eighteenth century. The basis of this ongoing engagement was the formulation of the discourse of the "society or "nation." Nation is then a historical reality, it has historical presence as it is spoken to by history, it speaks of history and it speaks in history. This historical reality is also a plural reality as it comprises persons of similarities that bind them together in a social order, therefore you speak of "nations" and the nobility is such one of the "nations." Foucault states: "The nation or rather 'nations,' or in other words the collections, societies, groupings of individuals who share a status, mores, customs, and a certain particular law-in the sense of regulatory statutes rather than statist laws." (Foucault 2003 pg. 134). The nations are then what constitutes history as they act, they speak to history and being distinct from each other, therein is created the continuum of actions and voices of history. Foucault states: "it is the nation that begins to speak. The nobility is one nation, as distinct from the many nations that circulate within the State and come into conflict with one another." (Foucault 2003 pg. 134). This is then the new historical knowledge of France, formulated and released in the run up to the Revolution, that was effectively embraced by all sides in the discursive ferment: sections of the nobility, the absolute monarchy, the bourgeoisie and the radical elements. The challenge it posed to the knowledge of the absolute monarchy resulted in an attempt in the run up to the Revolution to dominate this new historical knowledge, a sort of colonisation of knowledge. This new historical knowledge of the eighteenth century will then rise in the ferment to signal discursive lines – namely nationalism, race and class. Foucault states: "It is this notion, this concept of the nation that will give rise to the famous revolutionary problem of the nation; it will, of course give rise to the basic concepts of nineteenth century nationalism. It will give rise to the notion of race. And, finally, it will give rise to the notion of class." (Foucault 2003 pg. 134). This alternate historical knowledge did not present praises of power and its existing structures, rather it stressed on the dark side of power, power relations and the deeds of those exercising power, ensuring in eighteenth century France the groups in contention for power and hegemony all utilised this historical knowledge in the battles for ascendency. From the 1760s onwards the monarchy made a determined effort to subjugate this knowledge until its demise in the Revolution. Foucault states: "This is no longer the glorious history of power; it is the history of its lower depths, its wickedness, and its betrayals." (Foucault 2003 pg. 135). This discourse in its French form, problematizes power and the exercise of power, conjures up a new pathos that infects history and its interpretation, contributing to the creation of a specific from of right wing French political discourse. Foucault continues on the acceptability of the discourse in eighteenth century France as follows: "Just as the discourse circulated from Right to Left, from the nobiliary reaction to a bourgeois revolutionary project, so royal power tried to appropriate or control it." (Foucault 2003 pg. 136). This is then a discourse of grave political impact on the power relations of France in the eighteenth century and thereafter, especially in its formulation of race and class as aggregations of humanity in the tradition of its original formulation of nations, which is the forerunner concept. At this juncture the deconstruction of session seven follows.

Session Seven: 18 February 1976

France: Nation, Nobility and Historical Knowledge

In session seven Foucault continues with the genealogy of the historical discourse produced by the discursive agents of the French nobility in the seventeenth and eighteenth centuries. He begins his presentation by returning to the concept of the "nations" as follows: "But this vague, fluid, shifting notions of the nation, this idea of a nation that does not stop at the frontiers but which, on the contrary is a sort of mass of individuals who move from one frontier to another, through States, beneath States, and at the intra-State level, persists, long into the nineteenth century..." (Foucault 2003 pg. 142). The discursive agents of the French nobility engaged with the hegemonic discourse of the absolute monarchy formulated the concept that is the basis for the creation of a new concept of history, a new historical knowledge, a new conception of the social order and a new definition of power relations. The concept of nation will eventually lead to the conceptualisation of the discourse of war as the basis of the social order. The French nobility in its engagement with the absolute monarchy formulated and unleashed into the mass of statist historical discourse this most disruptive concept/principle, where the nation becomes the subject-object of history. A concept/principle that demanded a new history and a new conception of power relations in a social order. At the end of the seventeenth and the beginning of the eighteenth centuries the nobility found itself engaged on two fronts: one with the absolute monarchy over the issue of public right and the other with the Third Estate. The nobility was then forced to devise specific strategies to deal with entirely different realities of engagement. For the engagement with public right exercised by the monarchy, the nobility claimed freedom that was theirs as a result of the Frankish invasion and overthrow of the Roman Imperium. Against the Third Estate the nobility claimed the rights of invasion bestowed on the nobility, unlike the commoners of the Third Estate. The nobility found itself in eighteenth century France in a precarious position which demanded a new discursive formulation that enabled it to engage with two distinct terrains of engagement, demanding two distinct discourses simultaneously, resulting in the formulation of the discourse of war premised on the difference of nations. And in this journey through the evolution of the discourse Foucault focuses on the works of Boulainvilliers.

Boulainvilliers' Discourse of Race War

Boulainvilliers, as well as others, are involved in the task of creating a strategy for victory that is articulated by a discourse and its attendant worldview. The Boulainvilliers concept of freedom is instructive as it is rooted in a mythic presentation of the meaning of freedom to the Germanic/Frankish destroyers of the Roman imperium in Gaul. Foucault states: "The freedom of these warriors is not the freedom of tolerance and equality for all; it is a freedom that can only be exercised through dominance. Far from being a freedom based upon respect, it is, in other words, a freedom based upon ferocity." (Foucault 2003 pg. 148). Those who claim "freedom" inherited from the Germanic invasion must then understand, seek and exercise domination. Freedom that is ferocious and driven by ferocity in the quest for domination is valid freedom, anything else is less than valid and will be the basis of being dominated. The edifice that eventually was capped off with the discourse of war was being built from the foundation up. Foucault states: "A freedom that cannot be translated into a nonegalitarian relationship of force can only be a freedom that is weak, impotent, and abstract." (Foucault 2003 pg. 157). Being dominated by the absolute monarch has rendered the French nobility weak and impotent, thereby facilitating the assault of the Third Estate. Boulainvilliers insists that the submission of the nobility to the absolute monarchy was not attained with their loss in battle, but at the point in which the nobility surrendered discursively by not generating and releasing knowledge that serves the nobility. The nobility in the seventeenth and eighteenth centuries must now reassert themselves as vocal, active historical subjects in the order of knowledge. Foucault states: "So if it wishes to become a historical force, that implies that it must, in the first instance acquire a new self-awareness and reinsert itself into the order of knowledge." (Foucault 2003 pg. 155). The nobility has then to remake itself in the image and likeness of the Germanic-Frankish blond warriors by reimaging themselves via a new historical discourse of relevance to the terrain of engagement that is current. This reimaging, the production of knowledge and the assault on the order of knowledge are strategic necessities on the path to victory. Boulainvilliers completes the discursive edifice with his insistence that the dynamic of forces engaged in the battle for dominance in the social order must be understood, for it is the key to understanding the terrain of battle and the strategic imperative for victory. History is then a calculation of forces. In his quest to discover and understand the forces that make the weak strong and in other instances the strong weak, Boulainvilliers insisted that the force was the raging war that permeates the social order. Foucault states: "With Boulainvilliers, in contrast, we have a generalised war that permeates the entire social body and the entire history of the social body; it is obviously not the sort of war in which individuals fight individuals, but one in which groups fight groups." (Foucault 2003 pg. 162). Since there exists a continual state of war in the social order the dynamic of the calculation of forces of history is rooted in the capacity and preparedness of any and all groups for the specific war it is involved in at a specific point in time. Boulainvilliers has now arrived at the core concept of his discourse and that is the all-pervasive war between groups that drives the social order. This concept begets a specific formulation of history that accepts the fact of an all pervasive war in the social order and is analysed in terms of the all-pervasive war and is the key to unlock the mysteries of history. Foucault states: "A history that takes as its starting point the fact of war itself and makes its analysis in terms of war can relate all these things-war, religion, politics, manners, and characters-and can therefore act as a principle that allows us to understand history." (Foucault 2003 pg. 163). War then makes the social order knowable and understandable but from a specific discursive worldview which manufactures and moulds the reality it presents, as all discourses do.

Grid of Intelligibility

Foucault next in the session introduces in passing his concept of "grid of intelligibility." In this concept Foucault is insisting that even though one applies the duality of true/false to Boulainvilliers discourse and pronounce it either true or false these are in fact "demonstrations" of truth or falsehood which means that the discourse is intelligible, it resonates. Boulainvilliers has then created within his discourse this grid of intelligibility that enables judgment on its veracity, thereby establishing its discursive impact and the impact of all historical discourse that followed. For without the grid of intelligibility there is no historical discourse, there are only myths and legends with an alien regime of truth. The grid of intelligibility then dances with the hegemonic regime of truth which ensures the impact and influence of the power/knowledge nexus of its historical discourse. This makes historical discourse resonate with the listener. Foucault states: "When I speak of a grid of intelligibility, I am obviously not saying that what Boulainvilliers said is true. One could probably even demonstrate that everything he said was false. I am simply saying that it could be demonstrated." (Foucault 2003 pg. 163). Foucault continues on the seventeenth century discourse of the Trojan origin of the Franks and the emigration of the Franks from France to the rest of Europe as follows: "cannot be said to have anything to do with our regime of truth and error. In our terms, it is neither true nor false." (Foucault 2003 pg. 164). This discourse was not historical discourse as it had no grid of intelligibility, as it lacked a regime of truth and error of relevance to the present era. Discourse without this relevant regime has then to be absorbed into a current historical discourse in order for it to gain traction and relevance, as seen in the discourse of National Socialism in Germany. Foucault continues: "Boulainvilliers, in contrast, does, I think, establish a certain regime, a certain division between truth and error, that can be applied to Boulainvilliers's own discourse and that can say that his discourse is wrong-...The fact remains that it is this grid of intelligibility that has been established for our historical discourse." (Foucault 2003 pg. 164). Boulainvilleirs's historical discourse is then a historical discourse by dint of its grid of intelligibility, setting the standard for the formulation of future historical discourses thereafter.

Force Relations as a Historico-Political Object

Foucault in the closing stage of this session then presents his concept of force relations as a historico-political object invented by Boulainvilliers's discourse of war. When Boulainvilliers's discourse located force relations in a constant war between nations, whereby each nation other than the Sovereign can locate and place in its own history; then war and force relations become a historical object that is no longer the exclusive preserve of the Sovereign. Each nation traces and articulates its history of war and force relations between nations. By doing this it becomes a political act constituting war and force relations as an historico -political object. Each nation has then its own history, its own truth and falsehood that are instruments of war as these instruments are vital towards generating self-awareness of the members of the nation towards liberation. Foucault states: "The relationship of force now becomes a historical object that someone other than the sovereign-can locate and determine within its own history. The relationship of force, which was once an essentially political object, becomes a historical object, or rather a historico-political object..." (Foucault 2003 pg. 164). Force is no longer a public right or the exclusive power of the sovereign because the social order is driven by war, a historical object outside of the control of public right. Then force relations are also a historical object outside of the control of public right, as is history. With each nation visualising this historical object towards the prosecution of the war of the social order then war and force relations are historico-political objects. Force relations as an object of knowledge then constitutes a historico-political field which facilitates the blending of historical with political action. Foucault states: "At this point, it all comes together: History functions within politics, and politics is used to calculate historical relations of force." (Foucault 2003 pg. 164).

The Truth Matrix of Historical Discourse

Foucault then presents his concept of historical-discourse's truth-matrix. The discourse of war insists that the truth and the Logos does not begin with the end of violence but is created with, through and because of war between nations. The truth and Logos of the epoch were born with the launch of the war between the nobility, the sovereign and the Third Estate in France. War then gives birth to historical discourse and the truth-matrix of the discourse. A historical discourse determines truth and Logos of a specific typology distinct, separate and apart from that of the discourse of law and sovereignty and locked in a dance for dominance. The discourse then produces its own structure of truth with its mechanism and apparatuses of power that polices its truth, as all other discourses. Foucault states: "truth does not begin, or truth and the Logos do not begin, when violence ceases. On the contrary, it began when the nobility started to wage its political war against both the Third Estate and the monarchy, and it was in this war and by thinking of history in terms of war that something resembling what we now know as historical discourse could establish itself." (Foucault 2003 pg. 165). Next in the ending of the session Foucault assaults the position that history was invented by the bourgeoisie. The position states that the bourgeoisie as a rising class was rational and universal in its worldview, hence the only class in France and Europe capable of producing a rational and universal history. Foucault dismisses this position for him it is a cliché as it was the nobility at war with the sovereign and the Third Estate who created the historical discourse of war. The terrain of the engagement and the strategic imperative for victory demanded rational and universal conceptualisations of war, which then enabled the nobility to invent history though its historical discourse of war. The adulation of the bourgeoisie shared by Karl Marx and Max Weber is dismissed by Foucault as the inbred, decadent French nobility formulated and released the historical discourse of war, which was then adopted by the bourgeoisie and the proletariat; and in so doing invented the concept of rational, Universal history and historico-political historicism. Foucault states: "It was precisely because it was fighting a war that it was able to take war as an object, war being at once the starting point for the discourse, the condition of possibility for the emergence of a historical discourse, a frame of reference, and the object of that discourse." (Foucault 2003 pg. 165). The political war the nobility was engaged in with the sovereign and the Third Estate demanded a discursive approach to war where war is the object/subject of the discourse formulated. A rational, universalist discourse of war and for war predicated on the order created by the concept of nations at war and for war. Foucault states: "War was both this discourse's starting point and what it was talking about." (Foucault 2003 pg. 165).

Finally, Foucault ends this session with the statement that the position of Clausewitz on war and politics was possible because of the English historians and Boulainvilliers, who preceded Clausewitz by some two hundred years and one hundred years respectively, and their discourse of war. Where in the seventeenth century and at the beginning of the eighteenth century it was articulated and demonstrated that politics is the continuation of war by other means.

Foucault is therefore insisting that the decline of the absolute monarchy, the rise of the humanist secular society, the stripping of the political power of organised Christian religion and the tumult of the French Revolution, characterised by the rise of nationalism, racism and class warfare, were all made possible by the historical discourse of war and its historico-political historicism.

Session Eight: 25 February 1976

Force Relations, War and History

In session eight Foucault continues with the genealogy of Boulainvilliers's discourse by insisting that Boulainvilliers in fact created a historico-political field where he began to gaze upon power from the reality of those it is exercised upon, which resulted in the construction of the concept of forces to which power belonged. Boulainvilliers was then involved in writing a history of force relations of which a history of power relations was part of. Power relations are then relational and ever dynamic, which means that power cannot be possessed only exercised and it is not a form of might. Rebellion and war is the expressed form of might/violence, but that is also relational, therefore forming a continuum with power under the ambit of force relations. Power can then only be studied with reference to the terms of the power relations. Boulainvilliers by writing a history that defined the relational nature of power and analysed it in history then presented a challenge to the hegemonic discourse of law and sovereignty. This challenge of historical discourse changed the discursive terrain and the nature of the engagement; where political life and political knowledge begins to be written/inscribed on the force relations or the real struggle of the social order. The strategy of struggles indicated the use of historical knowledge in its formulation and articulation. This historical discourse then changed the nature of politics whilst it invented history. Foucault states: "I think that from the eighteenth century onward-and it is at this point that political life and political knowledge begin to be inscribed in society's real struggles-strategy, or the element of calculation inherent in such struggles, will be articulated with a historical knowledge that takes the form of the interpretation and analysis of forces." (Foucault 2003 pgs. 171-172). A unique discourse rooted in history that focused on force relations changed dramatically the nature of political struggle in France preparing the terrain for the Revolution and its aftermath. Foucault continues: "We cannot understand the emergence of this specifically modern dimension of politics unless we understand how, from the eighteenth century onward, historical knowledge becomes an element of the struggle: it is both a description of struggles and a weapon in the struggle. History gave us the idea that we are at war; and we wage war through history." (Foucault 2003 pg. 172). Foucault sums up the impact of this historical discourse of war through its redefinition of politics by its practise in a social order driven by war, which is the nature of modern politics: the pursuit of war by another means.

This historical discourse of war has then defined historicism, the basis of which is the link between war and history and between history and war, where war drives history and history is the basis of war. Historicism is averse to hegemonic discourse which drives an ongoing engagement between philosophy, scientific and political discourse. The basis of the engagement is the worldview constituted by historical discourse/historicism for it only sees, finds and analyses force relations and war that is never ending and the determinant of history and its subject matter: war. This never ending determinant of war constitutes its specific knowledge that is simply a weapon in a war, an instrument of a strategy of war. Foucault states: "historicism is nothing other than what I have just been talking about: the link, the unavoidable connection, between war and history, and conversely, between history and war." "historical knowledge never finds nature, right, order, or peace." "historical knowledge discovers only an unending war, or in other words forces that relate to one another and come into conflict with one another." (Foucault 2003 pgs. 172-173). Historical knowledge cannot escape the embrace of war, discover the basic laws of war or impose limits on war as it is the product of war, therefore it serves war, creating a steel circularity of inevitable war. Foucault states: "Knowledge is never anything more than a weapon in a war or a tactical deployment within that war. War is waged throughout history, and through the history that tells the history of war. And history, for its path, can never do anything more than interpret the war it is waging or that is being waged through it." (Foucault 2003 pg. 173). History is then the captive, even the hostage, of war. Is this the existential reality of humans aggregated into nations, races and classes?

Disciplinarisation of Knowledge

Foucault at this point in the session moves on to the concept of the "disciplinarisation" of knowledge. Foucault's presentation of this concept involves firstly treatment of the threat posed by historical discourse to hegemonic western discourse. Western hegemonic discourse defined itself by the stance that knowledge and truth inevitably are married to order and peace and that they cannot serve nor propagate violence, disorder and war. The threat posed by historical discourse was then real, palpable for the basis of this western nexus was the position that knowledge can only be truth and the obverse. All discourses deemed untrue are then not knowledges and must then be subjugated, absorbed, even disciplinarised; where a mechanism with its apparatuses of power/knowledge set about the task at hand of absorbing, silencing, subjugating and rendering these discourses objects of hegemonic discourse. Therefore, in eighteenth France towards the end of the 1780s the monarch Louis XVI set about the task of the disciplinarisation of the historical discourse through an organ of the State, the Ministry of Culture, which ended in spectacular failure. For the discourse now had multiple nations ascribing to its worldview by then, which gave impetus to especially the radical, and for that era the extremist, agenda of the Jacobins. The mechanism of disciplinarisation of knowledge in eighteenth France was then faced with its gravest threat and its most strategically important task in that century to date, which it botched. Foucault states on the Ministry of Culture as follows: "Its purpose was to arm the king for the political battle insofar as he was, after all no more than one force among others, and was being attacked by other forces. Its purpose was also to attempt to impose a sort of enforced peace on those historico-political struggles. Its purpose was to code this discourse on history once and for all, and in such a way that it could be integrated into the practice of the State." (Foucault 2003 pgs. 177-178). The base strategy is then to co-opt the discourse, pre-empting the challenge to hegemonic discourse, premised on absorption into the power/knowledge nexus of the State. Thereby creating a mechanism of power with its apparatuses of power characterised by the operational remnants of diverse absorbed discourses impacting and influencing the strategies of power, even though contradictory to the public discursive line of hegemonic discourse.

The Enlightenment and The Cognition-Truth Axis vs. The Discourse-Power Axis

In the session Foucault next presents his concept of the difference of the history of science and the genealogy of knowledges within the ambit of the problematic of the Enlightenment. Foucault states that the history of science is rooted in a continuum from cognition to the demand for truth, which he describes as the "cognition-truth axis", where the terminal stage of all cognition is the production and dissemination of truth, a truth and truths. The genealogy of knowledges in its opposition, its state of being "anti" is driven by and must be driven by a continuum that deconstructs, dismantles and lays bare the continuum of the cognition-truth axis. Foucault terms this insurrectionary device the discourse-power axis or the discursive practice-clash of power axis. Foucault's continuum is then premised on exposing the relationship between discourse and power in all its complexity. From the power/knowledge nexus to the mechanism and apparatuses of power of each discourse deployed in an engagement between contending discourses for hegemony, hence clash of power. Foucault states: "the history of sciences is essentially located on an axis that is roughly speaking, the cognition-truth axis, or at the least the axis that goes from the structure of cognition to the demand for truth." "the genealogy of knowledges is located on a different axis, namely the discourse-power axis or, if you like, the discursive practice-clash of power axis." (Foucault 2003 pg. 178).

But to deploy the discourse of discursive practice-clash of power and its mechanism and apparatuses of power it has to first falsify the discourse of the Enlightenment through engaging with it. For the discourse of the Enlightenment and its attendant history of science relentlessly seeks to disarm, to silence, to relegate and selectively absorb, therefore to "disciplinarise" the discourse of discursive practice-clash of power. Foucault states: "the genealogy of knowledge must first-before it does anything else-outwit the problematic of the Enlightenment." "when we look at the eighteenth century-we have to see...something very different: an immense and multiple battle...between knowledges in the plural-knowledges that are in conflict because of their very morphology, because they are in the possession of enemies, and because they have intrinsic power-effects." (Foucault 2003 pgs. 178-179). The genealogy of knowledges must then engage with the dualities of the discourse of the Enlightenment which insists that it is only with surrender to the discourse is human progress and prosperity possible, which is an attempt to mask the reality of power relations generated by this discourse. The very nature of discourse begets enemies, battles, engagement and the quest for hegemony, for these are the largesse of the power-effects of discourse. A discourse must be written on warm, cognitive bodies, it must constitute successive waves of warm, disciplined compliant cognitive bodies, for failure to accomplish these tasks potently indicate that it is but a subjugated, suppliant and supplicant knowledge. Not even a passing grade replicant. The imperative then is to exercise power, for failure to exercise power results in power being exercised on you. Discourse is an instrument devised by humans to attain a given, desired human end. Human desire then drives and places the limits to the entire process, for there are always limits to power.

Disciplines, Disciplined Knowledges Are Sciences

Foucault utilises a genealogy of technological knowledges in the eighteenth century to illustrate his concept of the disciplinarisation of knowledges or disciplinary power. Foucault states that there are four goals and four operations of disciplinary power or the disciplinarisation of knowledges. These are: selection, normalisation, hierarchicalisation and centralisation. These four operations driving the four goals strive to attain the strategic end of the disciplining of knowledges to become disciplines in the service of hegemonic discourse. A discipline exercised its own field and criteria of selection which enabled it to eradicate false knowledge or nonknowledge. Disciplined knowledge/discourse exercised forms of normalisation and homogenisation of the content of knowledge to ensure functional continuity across the spectrum of hegemonic discourse by disarming the challengers. There are forms of hierarchicalisation married to a central organisation that centralises a hierarchy of knowledges within hegemonic discourse. This centralised hierarchy of knowledges is held together in a matrix bonded by self-evident truths dispensed as axioms. This then was the basis of a disciplined knowledge in the eighteenth century, evolving into a discipline, which then produced a "science." Where, in this discipline/science knowledges have been disciplinarised from within, normalised and homogenised then centralised and hierarchicalised by a central organisation which ensures communication, continuity and discipline across the range of knowledges held in the field. The power wielded over the field is expressed via hegemonic axioms. This then is a science, which is an instrument of hegemonic discourse, charged with policing truth by producing discourses of truth that comply with the axioms of the field that constituted and drives this science. Foucault states: "Science in the singular did not exist before the eighteenth century. Sciences existed, knowledges existed, and philosophy, if you like existed." "The disciplinarisation of knowledges, and its polymorphous singularity, now leads to the emergence of a phenomenon and a constraint that is now an integral part of our society. We call it 'science.'" (Foucault 2003 pg. 182). The core of the disciplinarisation of knowledges is then a "polymorphous singularity" where a range and variety of knowledges, retrofitted and compliant knowledges, circulate around a central organisation held together by the powerful axioms that are its binding agent, the discursive agent forming a discursive singularity. Where all knowledges it encounters are absorbed and digested, where nothing escapes the path of the singularity and no light escapes from the singularity by dint of its axiomatic bond; hence Foucault's rejection of the Enlightenment project. Foucault states that before science, philosophy was the medium through which knowledges communicated with each other. Science banishes philosophy from its role in the communication of knowledges and brands it a nonscience, even an antiscience, relegating it to the margins of knowledges reserved for the marginalised. The same was done to the project for the formulation of a universal science (*mathesis*). Foucault states: "Science, defined as a general domain, as the disciplinary policing of knowledge, takes over from both philosophy and *mathesis*. From now on, it will raise specific problems relating to the disciplinary policing of knowledge: problems of classification, problems of hierarchicalisation, problems of proximity and so on." (Foucault 2003 pg. 182). Under the rubric of the progress of reason this dramatic change in the disciplinarisation of knowledges was being played out; and in this process of the disciplinarisation of polymorphous and heterogeneous knowledges a centralised, dominant and powerful apparatus of knowledges was created and operationalised. Part of this apparatus was the newly reformatted university whose allotted task was the selection of knowledges. This instrument of the apparatus of knowledge was charged with interrogating knowledges, determining their pedigree and marking them for exclusion from or inclusion into the grand apparatus of knowledge. This university is then a multioperational instrument of power, where it excludes and includes, accepts and rejects towards creating and policing a consensus, a field of knowledge and to homogenise knowledge forming a scientific community. These are all vital to the task of branding knowledges acceptable/unacceptable, truth/falsehood with authority, impact and believability akin to a cult following: the cult of science. Which means that the operations of this university involve the utilisation of the operations of State apparatuses to centralise knowledge, where the university and this State apparatus are in fact one and the same. The university is then contributing towards the task of centralising knowledges through the functions allocated to it by the State apparatuses. "Science" and "academia" are then elements of a discourse of truth devised by hegemonic discourse to mask the disciplinary power the university wields. Foucault points out that there is no mystery in the fact that this newly reformatted university appeared at the beginning of the nineteenth century, at the very time the disciplinarisation of knowledges into disciplines was taking place. Foucault states: "But from the end of the eighteenth and beginning of the nineteenth centuries onward-we see the emergence of something like a sort of great uniform apparatus of knowledges," "The university's primary function is one of selection...of knowledges." "that anything that exists outside it, any knowledge that exists in the wild, any knowledge that is born elsewhere, is automatically, and from the outset, if not actually excluded, disqualified a priori." (Foucault 2003 pg. 182). The role of this vassal of the centralised apparatus of knowledges is as follows: "Its role is to homogenise knowledges by establishing a sort of scientific community with a recognised status; its role is to organise a consensus. Its role is, finally, to use, either directly or indirectly, state apparatuses to centralise knowledges." (Foucault 2003 pg. 182).

A Change in the Form of Dogmatism

Foucault next presents the second phenomenon that resulted from the disciplinarisation of knowledges which was the change in the standard used to determine the truth/falsehood of statements with the removal of the old orthodoxy by a new, markedly different and antagonistic orthodoxy which Foucault terms: "a change in the form of dogmatism." The old orthodoxy of statements rooted in religious and ecclesiastical discourse therefore determined true/acceptable statements from untrue/unacceptable statements on the basis of Christian religious truths; which meant that statements that were true under the discourse of science were deemed untrue/unacceptable. The central operational mode of the old orthodoxy then was compliance to truth. The disciplinarisation of knowledges from the eighteenth century would establish an entirely different and antagonistic orthodoxy of statements rooted in the specific nature of the enunciation. This new orthodoxy ushers in dramatic change in the epistemology of Europe as the obstacles to the production and circulation of scientific truth endemic to the old orthodoxy were removed. This new orthodoxy was then vitally necessary to the progress of the scientific fields created by the disciplinarisation of knowledges. This new orthodoxy, with a new epistemology, fostered spaces in the enunciation of statements and its policing which might be termed "liberal": where ideas of nationalism, race, class and rights of the citizen and human rights were now part of the political language of the eighteenth century and thereafter. But this affording of "liberal" space was bolstered by and did support the operations of a much more efficient policing of the new orthodoxy. Foucault states that this new orthodoxy is then characterised by: "Who is speaking, are they qualified to speak, at what level is the statement situated, what set can it be fitted into, and how and to what extent does it conform to other forms and other typologies of knowledge." (Foucault 2003 pg. 184). The policing of statements is then rooted in fields of science and scientific knowledges where the speaker of the statement is under scrutiny, as well as the discursive content of the statement. Conformity with existing disciplinarised knowledges is then the basis for inclusion and the embrace of hegemonic discourse. Diversity, difference and rights are then mythic instruments of a discourse of truth. Foucault continues as follows: "We move, if you like, from the censorship of statements to the disciplinarisation of enunciations, or from orthodoxy to what I would call 'orthology', to a form of control that is now exercised on a disciplinary basis." (Foucault 2003 pg. 184).

68

Disciplinarised Knowledges, Disciplined Bodies

Finally, Foucault sums up this foray of his into his discourse of discipline and disciplinarisation to the human body and knowledges respectively. The application of the disciplines of power to the human body constituted the subjugated human body a specific type that is the object of power. These subjugated bodies generated knowledge and power was exercised over the subjugated body. But without the simultaneous development of the disciplinarisation project where knowledges are disciplinarised not bodies, where a new epistemology facilitates the expansion of scientific fields and their operations, the new mode of the relationship between power and knowledge will not have appeared and operationalised, ensuring the collapse of the scientific order, fields and the discourse that drives it. Which meant that there would have been no order of biopolitics. The new mode of power/knowledge, birthed by the simultaneous appearance and development of the discourses of disciplined bodies and disciplinarised knowledges, is the operational mode that made biopolitics a reality. The desire for docile bodies begets the need for disciplinarised knowledges by which to capture and render bodies docile. But only captured docile bodies can produce and apply the operational process necessary to disciplinarised knowledges. They then beget each other as there is no grand centralised human agency above the process, no master programmer/architect of the matrix. The ultimate expression of revolutionary action in this power/knowledge terrain is to be a discursive agent in the creation and operationalisation of a challenging, counter discourse that draws the assault of the mechanism and apparatuses of power, and pay the price thereof.

The Historico-Political Discourse vs. Disciplinarised History

At the end of the session Foucault returns to power relations between historical knowledge and hegemonic discourse during the eighteenth century. Historical knowledge engaged in a power struggle with hegemonic discourse was then subjected to an attempt to disciplinarise it, thereby turning it into a state discourse. The discourse of race war was then faced with the assault of disciplinarisation from various sources as the assault from reformatted historical discourses and other state discourses. The relentless assault failed to disciplinarise the discourse of race war, in fact it increased its potency, thereby creating the continuum of history and antihistory or a counter history locked in an ongoing engagement. Where this disciplinarised history, history as a discipline within its field of knowledge, is perpetually engaged with a historical knowledge that is in fact a political consciousness, a platform for specific political action that threatens hegemonic discourse. A recalcitrant historical knowledge that refuses to be disciplinarised, to be subjugated. The political struggle that historical knowledge was engaged in necessitated the development of history as an instrument in the political struggle, which meant that the relationship historical knowledge had with power in the eighteenth century changed dramatically. Historical knowledge was then excised from power to become an instrument in a political struggle. This was the political struggle mounted by the discourse of race war and its attendant specific historical knowledge. Historical knowledge reformatted by the State was then thrown into the political struggle with the discourse of race war in an attempt to disciplinarise it. Why did the attempt to reformat the discourse of war fail? Foucault did not provide an answer to this in this session. Foucault states: "Royal power's objective was to discipline historical knowledge, or historical knowledges, and thus to establish a State knowledge." "where historical knowledge is concerned, disciplinarisation did occur, but it not only failed to block the non-Statist history, the decentered history of subjects in struggle, but actually made it stronger thanks to a whole set of struggles, confiscations, and mutual challenges. And to that extent, you always have two levels of historical knowledge and consciousness, and the two levels obviously drift further and further apart." (Foucault 2003 pg. 186). All historical knowledges were subject to disciplinarisation in the eighteenth century, but the body of historical knowledges was not homogeneous and the historical knowledge constructed and expressed as the discourse of race war was the one that resisted disciplinarisation. The resulting two bodies of historical knowledges are forever locked in a political struggle which accounts for their division and continued existence. Foucault states: "So we have on the one hand a knowledge that has effectively been disciplinarised to form a historical discipline and on the other hand, a historical consciousness that is polymorphous, divided, and combative. It is simply the other side, the other face of a political consciousness." (Foucault 2003 pg. 186). The historical knowledge of the discourse of race war is genetically different from the historical knowledges that succumbed to disciplinarisation, for it is a political consciousness clothed in a historical consciousness constructed to further the political agenda which is the propelling of a specific nation, race and class to the point where they exercise power over their enemy nation, race and class. This political agenda concentrated on the aggregation and the individuals comprising the aggregation of both the enemy and the chosen of history creates the "decentered history of subjects in struggle." Which means that it must by design be polymorphous, diverse and divided. Making it a cumbersome historical knowledge to dissect and deconstruct for the purpose of reformatting, disciplinarisation given the nature and epistemology of disciplined knowledge in a field charged with the task at hand. This then points to the possibility of formulating a discourse and its knowledge capable of resisting, on a sustainable basis, hegemonic discourse of the North Atlantic.

Chapter Six
Session Nine: 3 March 1976
Historical Discourse and the Revolution

In this session Foucault presents the evolution of historical knowledge in the run up to the Revolution dealing with the formulation of key discursive concepts which signalled the evolutionary path the discourse of race war was now on. Historical discourse at this time has evolved into a discursive weapon available for use by all adversaries in the political struggles of France. Historical discourse was not a discourse formulated by the nobility for exclusive use by the nobility in its political struggles, it was not an ideology of or an ideological product of the nobility. From the work of Boulainvilliers to this stage historical discourse had undergone a process of evolutionary change which had intensified its polymorphic state, which ensured that it was never relegated to being the ideological product of and to serve a single aggregation/nation. It in fact evolves into a generalised discursive tactic. At the time of the Revolution this discursive tactic is deployed in three different fields of battle with three different directions, which demand three different tactics. These are: the field of battle of nationalities primarily concerned with languages – therefore the field of philology, the field of battle of social classes primarily concerned with economic domination – therefore the field of political economy and the field of battle of race primarily concerned with biological specifications and selection – therefore the field of biology, specifically the biology of race difference. Which means that historical discourse and the issue of the problematic posed by biology were by the Revolution joined at the hips. In the run up to the revolution contending forces in the French social order were then availing themselves of the discursive weapon and tactics offered by historical discourse because of the diversity and range of fields of knowledge this discourse was engaged with; such as philology, political economy, biology, language, labour and life illustrating its polymorphous nature by practice. Each contending faction, nation, class and race then fashioned this discursive weapon in their image and likeness articulated by discourse, but they all shared core, common elements. Which meant that the course of the Revolution entailed paths of extremism and extremist solutions; as the terrain of possible action and the courses of action as the discourse were polymorphic. A key element in this engagement of the Revolution was the discursive evolution of factions of the Third Estate, especially the bourgeoisie and those factions that were discursive agents of the discourse of race war. Foucault states: "Philology, political economy, biology, Language, labour, life. We will see all this being reinvested in or rearticulated around this historical knowledge and the tactics that are bound up with it." (Foucault 2003 pg. 190). The historical figure, the individual, will then be reinvented in the eighteenth century by the discourse of race war.

The discourse of race war in the eighteenth century evolves as a direct result of various discursive developments, one such development was the cobbling together of the discursive concept of the "constituent point" of politics and history as an order of force, not of law that is in equilibrium. This constituent point in equilibrium marries the constitution of politics and history to revolution, not to law, as the constitution is rooted in and defined by a relationship of force. This discursive construct then leads to the formulation of a cyclical philosophy of history premised on a circularity of history, characterised and driven by cycles. An order of force, not law, puts in place revolution as the constituent point of history and politics which constitutes a cyclical history. Foucault states: "This philosophy of history as philosophy of cyclical time becomes possible from the eighteenth century onward, or in other words, once the two notions of a constitution and a relationship of force become established." "So we have a pair, a link among three things: constitution, revolution, and cyclical history." (Foucault 2003 pg. 193).

The Savage and *Homo Economicus*

In the process of formulating discursive concepts Boulainvilliers and his successors openly rejected these discursive concepts of the hegemonic discourse of juridical law and public right, namely: nature and the natural man, the savage, Homo economicus and the social contract. The alternate discursive concept was the barbarian. The discourse which stated that the savage, the natural man emerged from nature to create society via contract is engaging with the centrality of domination, force in the erection of the human social order in the discourse of race war for hegemony. This discourse of the savage as creator of human civilisation is using the savage creator as the originator of the social contract as the basis of law and sovereignty, of human rights and the juridical subject, a discourse of one segment of the European bourgeoisie. The discourse of *Homo Economicus* (in the 20th and 21st centuries this is neoliberal discourse) is the product of another segment of the European bourgeoisie where the human is a pure economic actor devoting his life to exchange/production/trading and barter which creates a dichotomy of useful/useless human action and actors, thereby extolling domination and force but entirely and only in an economic context, in the context of the generation of wealth. This discourse of *Homo Economicus* must be rejected by the discourse of race war as it is anathema to the core discursive concepts of this discourse. The reason why is obvious as it is a discourse devised by the opponents of the discourse of race war to dull the impact of this discourse in the war of the discourses as it denies that the social order is premised on an order of force, as the natural man/the savage is a social animal given to the formation of an order by consent and contract, and the *Homo Economicus* is a rational actor solely driven by exchange and barter, not an order of force. Foucault states: "What the historico-political discourse of Boulainvilliers and his successors is trying to ward off is both the savage who emerges from his forests to enter into a contract and found society, and the savage *Homo Economicus* whose life is devoted to exchange and barter. The combination of the savage and the exchange is, I think basic to juridical thought, and not only to eighteenth century theories of right-we constantly find the savage-exchange couple from the eighteenth century theory of right to the anthropology of the nineteenth and twentieth centuries." (Foucault 2003 pg. 194). In its battle for hegemony with hegemonic discourse of the eighteenth century the discourse of race war was compelled to oppose and discard the discursive constructs of the natural man/the savage who is both a creator of a social order premised on the contract and a pure economic actor/being simultaneously. What Foucault reveals is that the basic discursive construct of European post war neoliberalism is the product of hegemonic European discourse of law and sovereignty. The political cult of neoliberalism of the 20th and 21st centuries in the North Atlantic, is then the product of a discursive construct of hegemonic discourse becoming overdetermined by dint of this political cult, which has now effectively weakened the State and the mechanism and apparatuses of biopolitics. The savage/exchange coupling has then impacted knowledges and constituted fields of disciplines in Europe from the 18th to the 21st centuries. In the 20th century the formation of the political cult of neoliberalism was then the product of the scientific fields of disciplines constituted by neoliberalism, e.g. – the Chicago School, now making the grab for hegemonic power. The marriage between neoliberalism and so-called populist politics in the 21st century is not between neoliberalism and adherents of the discourse of race war in a 21st century context. This is a marriage between the products of the Enlightenment, the constituent parts of North Atlantic hegemonic discourse namely: neoliberalism, fascism and national socialism. This so-called populist politics is the marriage of neoliberalism to neo fascists and neo Nazis. They are both 'neo' as they are now subjugated knowledges, disciplinarised knowledges of North Atlantic hegemonic discourse, i.e. – nothing new, discursive streams that engaged with the discourse of race war for hegemony, disciplinarised knowledges forming the structure of knowledge of power, of the State, discourse and knowledges as instruments of power to ensure the sustainability of the order of power of the social order, just business as usual. Today they have openly embraced the centrality of domination and force in the discourse of race war, in their bid to ensure the hegemony of the oligarchic order spawned by the neo-liberal order which brings into ridicule the discourse of law and sovereignty. Their discursive moorings are no longer those of the discourse of race war, but those of hegemonic white supremacy. On the savage Foucault states: "the savage is essentially a man who exchanges. He is the exchanger: he exchanges rights and he exchanges goods. Insofar as he exchanges rights, he founds society and sovereignty. Insofar as he exchanges goods, he constitutes a social body which is, at the same time an, an economic body. Ever since the eighteenth century, the savage has been the subject of an elementary exchange." (Foucault 2003 pgs. 194-195). The so-called populist politicians of the 21st century North Atlantic are then proponents of the noble, neoliberal savage with a specific race and ethnicity: white power. They are then the solution to the threat to hegemonic discourse posed by a range of challengers, including Islam and non-white tsunamis of migrants.

The Barbarian and Historico-Political Discourse

The historico-political discourse of race war in its engagement with hegemonic discourse formulates and releases its counter construct to the noble savage defined by exchange. This is the construct of the barbarian. The barbarian is only a barbarian as long as a civilisation exists, i.e. – she/he is not of necessitating the waging of war and the destruction of that civilisation. The existential state of barbarism ends when all civilisation is destroyed, therefore all barbarians are compelled to invade and destroy all civilisations in existence. There is no exchange, no contract and no *Homo Economicus* for there can only be domination, war and destruction. As the existence of civilisation brings into being the barbarian for they are a duality locked in power/force relations premised on domination, war and conquest. A historical circularity that speaks to cycles and hints at the dialectic. This barbarian cannot then be the living expression of, the receptacle of, exchange in the natural order. The freedom of the barbarian is never exchanged in order to found the society, for the barbarian destroys in order to seize and maintain her/his freedom. The barbarian refuses to be the *Homo Economicus* for what they desire they seize by dint of force of arms, by warfare, simply then by domination, there is no exchange only domination in all its expressive diversity. Both discourses then locked in battle encounter logistical problems with their constructs: as the noble savage denies domination and power relations as the discourse insists that the savage loves order and peace above personal desire and freedom, therefore the social order is in fact a totality that encompasses its parts; and its parts willingly surrender personal freedom to ensure the integrity of the totality; whilst the discourse of race war, with its construct of the barbarian, focuses solely on domination and the grave problematic of creating and maintaining a social order across time in light of this domination and the penchant for war. This discourse then only sees might/ force and cannot envisage power relations, which influences the constructs formed for the creation of a social order, its governance and its sustainability. The historico-political discourse in the eighteenth century encompasses the four constructs of Boulainvilliers: constitution, revolution, barbarism and domination; which generate different combinations of constructs used and various emphases placed, depending on the groups in eighteenth century France utilising the discourse in their political wars for hegemony. Foucault insists that from the eighteenth to the twentieth centuries the grave problem was revolution *and* barbarism for all adherents to a historical knowledge or the historico-political discourse. This construct when articulated to its furthest extent then presented problems to the construction of the constituent point/constitution. What is the basis of the social order rooted in revolution and barbarism and can it generate a civilisation that does not beckon the assault of barbarians? Can domination be ended, thereby abolishing the nexus with revolution? Are revolution and barbarism inextricably linked? Can there be a social order without a civilisation generated? And the questions are endless. On the construct of the barbarian Foucault states: "The barbarian cannot exist without the civilisation he is trying to destroy and appropriate." "He does not make his entry into history by founding a society, but by penetrating a civilisation, setting it ablaze and destroying it." "The barbarian is essentially the vector for something very different from exchange: he is the vector for domination." (Foucault 2003 pg.195). Foucault states: "The type of history established by Boulainvilliers in the eighteenth century is, I think, that of the figure of the barbarian." (Foucault 2003 pg. 196). Boulainvilliers's entire project, and those that followed, was summed up in the construct of the barbarian as all what the discourse said the barbarian was and was not summed up the discourse and projected an image of the discourse. Which stirred human interpretation by those impacted by the discourse, especially hegemonic discourse seen in the dialectic of the savage vs the barbarian, the good versus the evil. On the problems generated by the four constructs of the historico-political discourse Foucault states: "I think that in the eighteenth century, the whole set of historical discourses is overshadowed by this problem: not revolution *or* barbarism, but revolution *and* barbarism, or the economy of barbarism in the revolution." (Foucault 2003 pg. 198).

The problem is then revolution *and* barbarism and Foucault lists three instruments devised to filter or redefine barbarism and formulate a history of barbarism, and France, thereof in an attempt to rescue the project from the conundrum generated by the constructs borrowed from Boulainvilliers. The third instrument is the most effective instrument as it armed the bourgeoisie and the Third Estate of France for the engagement with the monarchy and the nobility, which culminated in the French Revolution. The base established by Boulainvilliers speaks to a blond barbarian as a historical fact, the invasion of blond barbarians as a historical and juridical fact, the seizure of land and the enslavement of humans by the blond barbarian invaders and the creation of very limited royal power as a result. This is the base schemata created by Boulainvilliers that remains the base of the discourse thereafter. Already in this base schemata a race classification has appeared that will be further developed as the discourse evolves across time. National Socialism will speak of the Aryan Germanic barbarian superman, the master race. The first instrument devised is that of the monarchy, where the history devised is assaulting the position that the nobility are the heirs of the blond barbarian horde. The horde simply disappeared leaving space for the development of the absolute monarchy, which insists that the absolute monarchy is not the heir of the horde. The second instrument mirrors that of the instrument of Boulainvilliers, but it is now insisting that the freedom of the barbarian invader was bequeathed to Gaul in the form of a democracy, a barbarian democracy of the broadest kind, simply because they were barbarians. This then is the legacy of the barbarians to France: the rejection of and the battle against absolutism and domination. The third instrument presents a duality of barbarisms; where the Germanic barbarity is bad, rejected and malevolent which France has to be liberated from, and there is the good barbarism of the Gauls which is the real source of freedom and as such must be liberated from German barbarism. The basis of aggressive, jingoistic nationalism was then laid in the third instrument. This instrument dismantles the link between freedom and the Germanic invasion made by Boulainvilliers and the link between Roman hegemony over Gaul and absolutism is dismantled.

What must be envisaged is the potency of a process where hegemonic discourse adopts selected discursive constructs from the discourse of race war to produce a reformulated and reformatted discourse on the hunt for hegemony in France. This was the case of the bourgeois quest for hegemony

France: The Bourgeoisie and Hegemony

This instrument embraced by bourgeois historians in the nineteenth century now locates the germ of French freedom in Roman Gaul. The discourse of this instrument states that Gallic freedom flourished under Roman hegemony over Gaul, specifically in the urban centres of Roman Gaul. Roman absolutism then did not hinder or prevent the development of Gallic freedom and enterprise in the urban centres of Roman Gaul. This urban freedom and enterprise survived the Germanic invasion and the onset of feudalism that followed, concentrating their presence in the free towns. The gravest threat to urban freedom and enterprise was posed by the Germanic invasion and the feudal social order that followed in the wake of Germanic destruction of Roman Gaul/Pax Romana. The Third Estate embraced this third instrument with relish as it articulated a worldview that resonated with the insecurity of the Third Estate in the social order in the run up to the Revolution. This discourse then undertakes the task of constituting the Third Estate in resonance with its discursive constructs and its attendant worldview. This is a Third Estate that is now presenting its credentials for hegemonic power, justified via a revisionist formulation of Roman absolutism as the basis for a unique Gallic freedom and enterprise, the noble savage and *Homo Economicus* combined, rooted in the urban environment. The pedigree of the bourgeoisie/Third Estate to exercise hegemonic power flows then from Roman absolutism over Gaul. Roman absolutism over Gaul then created the basis for a liberal Roman hegemonic order, and by extension the bourgeoisie/Third Estate the inheritors of, the product of this liberal Roman hegemonic order, to replicate over eighteenth century France. By this discursive position the bourgeoisie potently illustrates its willingness, even its tendency, to embrace absolutism when freedom challenges its hegemony. It is a liberal order when it works to the benefit of the bourgeoisie. Foucault states: "we have a thesis which, will become the thesis of the Third Estate, because this is the first time that the history of the town, the history of urban institutions, and the history of wealth and its political effects could be articulated within a historical analysis. This history creates, or at least begins to create, a Third Estate that is a product not merely of the concessions granted by the king, but of its own energy, its wealth, its trade, and of a highly sophisticated urban law that is in part borrowed from Roman law, but which is also articulated with the freedom of old, or in other words, the Gaulish barbarism of old." (Foucault 2003 pg. 205). The discourse is charged with two tasks, which demands two broad strategies. Firstly, it has to convince the Third Estate of its special superior qualities, its ancestral historical legacy and its strategic place/position in the social order that constitute its fitness to rule. The Third estate has then to be conditioned to aggressively insist on and seek power, as they are uniquely outfitted to rule by history. Power is their entitlement and theirs alone. They are then the liberal nobility of the Roman hegemony over Gaul, fit and able to now rule France in the eighteenth century. Secondly, the discourse has to also convince the "others" that the bourgeoisie is in fact fit, able and raised up by history to rule over them in France. You simply cannot make the bid for power as a coherent social group, whether nation or class, until you have been constituted such by a historical discourse. Until such time the political actions undertaken will reflect the adventurism of fragments and factions in transition to becoming a group defined and policed by a hegemonic discourse. Foucault continues: "The bourgeoisie will be able to recuperate-in the form of the Gallo-Roman *municeps*-a Romanity that supplies, so to speak, its letters of nobility. The Gallo-Roman municipality is the Third Estate's nobility." "on the eve of the Revolution, Romanity can also lose all the monarchist and absolutist connotations it had had throughout the eighteenth century. A liberal Romanity became possible, and even those who are not monarchists or absolutists can revert to it. Even the bourgeois can revert to Romanity. And as you know, the Revolution will have no hesitation in doing so." (Foucault 2003 pg. 206).

Tactical Reversibility of Discourse and the Extra Discursive

Discourses in an engagement must then be able to allow a diversity of speakers articulating a diversity of tactical positions that are understandable and actionable across discursive lines. A field of knowledge that supports and enables this discursive engagement must then exist in order for the power relations to be produced and acted upon, as without understandability across discursive and tactical strategic lines there are no power relations, only force/might/violence. Foucault's construct to describe this reality is "the tactical reversibility of the discourse", where contending discourses articulated by speakers and actions are separated by strict lines of confrontation which enables a single discourse to adopt the functions of multiple tactical units within overall strategies. There is then no single strategic function or intent of a discourse locked in discursive confrontation. This is the result of various factors, namely: the nature of the homogeneity of the field of knowledge in which the discourse was formed, then there is the quality of the epistemological field that informs the field of knowledge and the homogeneity of the discourse's mode of formation. Foucault makes two statements of grave impact on this issue, namely: that overall strategies in which discourses function as different tactical units is multifaceted as they encompass discourse and truth or discourses of truth, power, status and economic interests. The tactical polyvalence of discourses in effect means the capacity of discourses within an overall strategy addressing all of the units of the overall strategy in all its diversity. This only arises within a field of knowledge with the required epistemological rigor, the requisite homogeneity of its content and the mode of formation of the discourse. Which points to the integrity of the process of the disciplinarisation of knowledge towards creating a field of knowledge, a relevant epistemology and the attendant discourse. In the second statement of grave impact Foucault insists that this entire process of the tactical reversibility of discourse is only successful when discourse is an effective tactical instrument in struggles that are extradiscursive. Discourse that is incapable of effectively impacting struggles in the realm of the extradiscursive then is discourse that has failed to breach the walls of the gravest test of being a tactically reversible discourse or a tactically polyvalent discourse. A discourse that can address, grapple with and impact any struggle in the realm of the extradiscursive, is a discourse that engages with power exercised where there is no need for discourse, where power is exercised between two or more individuals where there is no need for discourse, discursive constructs and an overall strategy at the base local level, possibly with a subjugated knowledge in operation devoid of a field of knowledge, an epistemology, a discourse and an overarching strategy. Tactically competent discourse must be able to link this extradiscursive base local level power relation into a chain of power relations that eventually form the institutions of the macro level. Without this chain effect, power relations will not be contained in discursive structures that enable an overall strategic agenda by which some order is brought to the mass of power relations in order to realise the macro, terminal expressions of power or the State. Foucault states: "The tactical reversibility of the discourse is, in other words, directly proportional to the homogeneity of the field in which it is formed. It is the regularity of the epistemological field, the homogeneity of the discourse's mode of formation, that allows it to be used in struggles that are extradiscursive." (Foucault 2003 pg. 208). Foucault then makes an important statement on the historico-political field as follows: "That, then, is the methodological reason why I emphasised that the different discursive tactics are distributed across a historico-political field that is coherent, regular and very tightly woven." (Foucault 2003 pg. 208). The historico-political field of the eighteenth century was then producing discourse that was tactically reversible or tactically polyvalent and it is necessary to methodologically understand this, for failure to understand this means that the impact of this discourse on power and the extradiscursive in the eighteenth century will never be unearthed, exposed.

Bourgeois Political Opportunism

As the session ends Foucault deals with the evolution of the political stance of the bourgeoisie as it moved from its antihistorical stance to a historical stance in the eighteenth century, specifically in the run up to the Revolution. In the first half of the eighteenth century the bourgeoisie articulated its preference for an enlightened despot. Where absolutism was moderated by knowledge, philosophy, technology and administration of a field of knowledge and a discourse that was not a historical knowledge, much less the historico-political discourse of race war. In the second half of the eighteenth century, especially in the run up to the Revolution, the bourgeoisie changed to an ahistorical position by demanding a constitution driven by the embrace of the construct of natural right and a form of the social contract. In response to the challenge mounted by the discourse of race war the bourgeoisie was now consorting with the discursive constructs of Rousseau, which illustrated their aversion to historicism and the politics derived thereof. But with the calling of the Estates General the nobility takes advantage of the moment to file a flood of grievances framed by historical discourses forcing the bourgeoisie to now follow suit. In response to the threat the bourgeoisie now launched its journey to create historical constructs, a bourgeois discourse of history or bourgeois historicism to engage with the enemy. Foucault states: "The Rousseauism of the bourgeoisie at the end of the eighteenth century, before and during, the Revolution, was a direct response to the historicism of the other political subjects who were fighting in the field of theory and political analysis. Being a Rousseauist, appealing to the savage and appealing to the contract, was a way of escaping an entire landscape that had been defined by the barbarian, his history, and his relationship with civilisation." (Foucault 2003 pg. 209). The bourgeoisie situated itself within the arms of the hegemonic discourse of law and sovereignty, which means that when the strategic imperative demanded the framing of a historical discourse primarily for the political wars disciplinarised historical knowledge was used. The bourgeoisie of France by the late eighteenth century was then situated within the ambit of hegemonic state discourse involved in the quest to displace the nobility from its social position in order to exert some form of hegemony over the social order, based on a working compromise with the monarchists. When events unfolded in the wake of the power relations of the Revolution the bourgeoisie ensured it was so placed to exploit such events to its advantage, such as the purge of the monarchists and the nobility.

Historicism, Race and Race Nationalism

Foucault states that during the course of the Revolution a number of historical forms or moments impacted the Revolution as the impact was seen in the vocabulary, institutions, signs, manifestations and festivals of the Revolution. These impacts enabled the visualisation of the Revolution as part of a cycle that had returned. Foucault presents two historical forms or moments he considers of strategic importance. One is the reformulation of the Roman city, of an archaic Rome that was republican and virtuous. The Gallo-Roman city of freedom and prosperity was now dumped, discarded and Roman festivals rooted in political ritualisations of freedom and virtue were adopted. This new Roman discursive architecture was married to the historical form of Charlemagne and the Carolingian model. Charlemagne, the sovereign-warrior, the protector of trade and the urban centres, both Germanic king and Roman emperor. The Charlemagne/Carolingian moment will deeply impact the course and form of the Revolution where this moment coalesces with the moment of the archaic Roman city in the Napoleonic Empire. The second historical moment of grave impact was the moment or historical form driven by the execration, demonisation of feudalism, which is obviously a construct designed as a political weapon, instrument in a war. This discourse of the execration of feudalism has multiple forms, illustrating a polyvalent discourse engaged in battle in the power relations of the trenches in the quest for hegemony. This is an in your face political discourse. This discourse creates a revisionist position on the invasion of the Germanic hordes of Gaul and their subsequent hegemony over Gaul. The discourse speaks to French nationalism defined in race terms, where the Germanic invaders are rejected on the basis of being foreign invaders of Gaul. They are not Gauls racially, they are then an invasive foreign race that dominated Gaul and left a legacy in France that must also be rejected, i.e. the nobility and the monarchy. There is then no right of conquest and no public right stemming from conquest by a foreign alien race, for nation, nationalism and the state were now expressions of the majority race, i.e. – the French. The discourse of race war by the Revolution had now set in motion the discursive momentum to formulate and apply discourses of race, nationalism and the State, not only in the context of Europe, but in the context of the world and the colonial project which was well under way at the time of the Revolution. The discourse of white supremacy was therefore the product of this discursive ferment in the run up to and during the Revolution. Foucault states: "I refer to the reactivation, during the Revolution itself, of a certain number of moments or historical forms that function as, if you like, the splendours of history. Their reappearance in the Revolution's vocabulary, institutions, signs, manifestations, festivals made it possible to visualise it as a cycle and a return." (Foucault 2003 pg. 210). New discourses that reformulated history were released in the political wars with the attendant impact on power relations and the formation and policing of knowledge. These power struggles so impacted the Revolution and its evolution that they defined the identity, the language and the worldview of the Revolution into a historical event rooted in a cycle of past and future events of history that repeat themselves. The Revolution was a historical event constituted by a historical cycle, which allowed the use of the past to define action and worldviews in the Revolutionary present. The Revolution was then the product of historicism. Foucault presents his analysis of one of the outcomes of the two dominant moments that impacted the Revolution as follows: "What we see taking shape here will be just as important in the early nineteenth century: The French Revolution-and the political and social struggles that went on during it-are being reinterpreted in terms of the history of races." (Foucault 2003 pg. 211). One outcome of the Revolution is the discourse of race as a historical knowledge, where history is interpreted by a discourse of race and race war is the driving force of history. This discourse of race is then the founding discursive core for the discourse of white supremacy, which was formulated in a discursive environment supposedly driven by liberty, egality and fraternity or the discourse of truth of revolutionary order. The bourgeoisie within the political struggles of the Revolution, is best placed to benefit from this new political weapon and therefore to contribute to its discursive formulation and release, especially in light of the Haitian Revolution, the issue of slavery and its re-imposition in the French colonial project.

Foucault speaks to the discursive battle over feudalism that raged during the entire eighteenth century in France. A battle at the level of knowledge and forms of power which impacted the imaginary of the French social order, seen in its fixation with the Gothic form. This battle heightened in the run up to and during the Revolution as the conjuncture spoke to the unfolding of a new hegemonic order. Hence the formulation and release of discourses of political assault premised on the demonisation of feudalism and its legacy, and the writing and popularity of gothic novels. These forms of expression are then symptomatic of the raging war then at the level of the power relations of the French social order. Power relations which impacted the course of the Revolution when unfurled. This demonisation of feudalism and its impact on the social order drove the power relations and the production of knowledges to the conjuncture that manifested publicly as the French Revolution. Foucault states: "The whole of the eighteenth century was obsessed with the problem of feudalism at the level of right, history, and politics. And it was only at the time of the Revolution-or a hundred years after all that work had been done at the level of knowledge and the level of politics-that there was finally a taking up again of these themes, at the level of the imaginary, in these science-fiction and politics-fiction novels. It was in this domain, therefore, that you had the gothic novel." (Foucault 2003 pg. 212). The demonisation of feudalism drives power relations that are acute, intense and grave, to the extent where they impact the imaginary. The execration of feudalism from the eighteenth to nineteenth centuries drove the evolution of the historico-political discourse, illustrated by the formulation and evolution of race nationalism and the impact on the imaginary, expressed through the Gothic form. On this point Foucault ends session nine.

Chapter Seven

Session Ten: 10 March 1976

The Embourgeoisement of the Discourse of Race War

This is the penultimate session of Michel Foucault's public lecture for 1976 at the College de Paris. At the commencement of the tenth session Foucault states that in the eighteenth century it was only the discourse of history that utilised war to analyse political relations, unlike the discourse of rights and the discourse of political theory. But from the Revolution onwards war, and its use as a tool of analysis, was either effectively eliminated from the discourse of history or effectively silenced or disciplinarised. Specifically, the construct of war without end in the social order and the construct of domination as the prime explanatory construct of the discourse of history were specifically targeted and gutted. Permanent war and domination were then replaced with the quest for reconciliation which was an inversion of the problem of war. Clearly in the aftermath of the Revolution the discourse of war was gutted to now speak and police a bourgeois worldview. This historical knowledge was now a discourse in the quest for bourgeois hegemony over the social order. Foucault states: "And it is this twofold threat-a war without end as the basis of history and the relationship of domination as an explanatory element in history-that will, in the historical discourse of the nineteenth century, be lessened, be broken down into regional threats and transitory episodes, and retranscribed in the form of crises and violence." (Foucault 2003 pgs.215-216). War is redefined as crises and violence that are specified regionally as transitory expressions of transitory crises and violence. There is no constant state of war driving politics in the social order, and violence and crises can be pinned on difference: regional, ethnic, race, nationalism and gender. Foucault continues: "What is more important still is, I think, the fact that this danger is essentially, destined to fade away in the end, not in the sense that we will attain the good and true equilibrium...but in the sense that reconciliation will come about." (Foucault 2003 pg. 216). The possible outcome of this new discourse is not a state of equilibrium that is "good" but reconciliation, which is an end vastly different to that of the eighteenth century discourse of race war. Reconciliation destroys the constructs of permanent war and domination. What then is the mechanism utilised to gut the discourse of race war of its two driving discursive constructs? For Foucault this was a self-inflicted process of internal dialecticalisation, which in fact was the instrument of the embourgeoisement of the discourse of race war. Foucault is then insisting that bourgeois discursive agents formulated the construct of the dialectic, which effectively dismantled the discourse of race war, reformulating it into a discourse in the service of the bourgeois quest for hegemony over the social order. Foucault states: "I think that what occurred was something like an internal dialecticalisation, a self dialecticalisation of historical discourse, and there is an obvious connection between this and its embourgeoisement." (Foucault 2003 pg. 216). With the reformulation of the discourse of race war, which banished at best the core constructs of perpetual war and domination, how is the construct of war reformulated and to what purpose? The new war is now a precondition for the survival of society in its political relations as the war is fought internally against threats that emerge from within the social order. These threats then arise from the organic nature and body of the social order, not history, but the biology of the social order. Race, deviance, physical and mental challenges and moral weakness are then the threats that demand this internal war. Racism, white supremacy, eugenics and moral rearmament were all apparatuses of power unleashed in prosecution of this internal bio/medical war. Foucault states: "war is no longer a condition of existence for society and political relations, but the precondition for its survival in its political relations. At this point, we see the emergence of an idea of the internal war that defends society against threats born of and in its own body. The idea of social war makes, if you like, a great retreat from the historical to the biological, from the constituent to the medical." (Foucault 2003 pg. 216). Threats emanating from the organic body must be identified and policed by hegemonic discourse and its mechanism and apparatuses of power; which brings into being the 'gaze' upon the members of the organic body and the formulation of a new power/knowledge nexus rooted in knowledge/power applied to, focused on the human body. The birth of biopolitics. Historical knowledge/the discourse of race war was not formulated to construct this new discourse with its attendant power/knowledge nexus.

But what this new discourse did was give more and more space within the boundaries of the discourse to evolve a series of new racist constructs which would present opportunities for the rise of knowledges that combined facets of the discourse of race war within this bourgeois discourse. This discourse also gave space to constructs of the once hegemonic discourse of public right and law and sovereignty to evolve and eventually capture the discipline of economics and political power relations. This is the construct of the noble savage and *Homo Economicus*. Hegemonic discourse that developed from the nineteenth century therefore carries constructs of the discourse of law and sovereignty, constructs of the discourse of race, racism and white supremacy and constructs of the discourse of *Homo Economicus,* which with other constructs are used to mask power relations where the so-called sovereign individual, the bearer of human rights is a subject of power that establishes force relations on definitions of difference as race, gender, sexual preference, physical and mental abilities, class and status.

Foucault next presents his analysis of the auto-dialecticalisation and embourgeoisement of historical discourse. Foucault posits that the basis of the embourgeoisement of historical discourse was premised on the reformulation of the construct of the 'nation' as formulated by the discursive agents of the nobility in the eighteenth century, where the 'a nation' evolved into 'the nation' which is in fact 'the State.' A political discourse was constructed which was Statist in focus where the State was now centralised and dominant. Foucault states: "that political reworking of the nation, of the idea of the nation, that led to the transformation that made a new type of historical discourse possible." (Foucault 2003 pg. 217). The nation can only exist when the right and necessary group, existing and functioning in a nation, exercises hegemony over the social order and sets in train the process of formulating the State which brings into being the nation. The group so chosen and destined to constitute the State, and by extension the nation, is the bourgeoisie or in the case of eighteenth century France the Third Estate. Before bourgeois hegemony there only existed forms of government that alluded to the possibility of the formulation of the State incapable of constituting the nation. This bourgeois group active in a nation in the domain of the *Homo Economicus* is the only group within a nation with the capacity to found the State. The bourgeoisie is then the product of *Homo Economicus,* as is the State that they constitute. Foucault states: "Where, then, are we to find the historical core of a nation that can become 'the' nation? In the Third Estate and only in the Third Estate. The Third Estate is in itself the historical precondition for the existence of a nation, but that nation should, by rights, coincide with the State. The Third Estate is a nation. It contains the constituent elements of a nation." (Foucault 2003 pgs. 221-222). The nation and the State is the artifice of the bourgeoisie, the instrument and expressions of its hegemony. Foucault lists two characteristics of this new political discourse of the bourgeoisie. First is the new formulation employed articulating a new relationship between particularity and universality, where the bourgeoisie is insisting that it recognises the functional operationality of other groups/nations in the social order but the other nations must recognise the unique reality of the bourgeoisie as the only, singular vehicle for progress, later modernity, amongst all the nations of the social order. Only the bourgeoisie is capable of ushering in the era of Statist universality through the totalist functioning of the State. Those nations seeking to partake in this State centred nirvana of universality must then allow the bourgeoisie the space and power to act. The bourgeoisie was then selling the three card hustle. The second characteristics of this new political discourse is its new formulation of the demand. The new demand is rooted not in the past, in history but in a bright, new, progressive future, later termed modernity, rooted in Statist universality. The bourgeoisie is then defined by their discourse of Statist universality. Foucault states: "The matrix of this political discourse, displays, I think, two characteristics. First, a certain new relationship between particularity and universality, a certain relationship which is precisely the opposite of that which characterised the discourse of the nobiliary reaction." "Perhaps we are not, in ourselves, the totality of the social body, but we are capable of guaranteeing the totalising function of the State. We are capable of Statist universality." (Foucault 2003 pg. 222). The bourgeoisie are the path to the universality of the State thereby creating the totality of the society, the social order. This totality is only possible through the operationalisation of the State and only the bourgeoisie can accomplish this. There was no Statist universality and no totality possible before the existence and actions of the bourgeoisie. The bourgeoisie has then no claim to historical precedence, its only claim is to progress then modernity. The bourgeoisie claims a public right premised on its sole ability to ensure a future. On the second characteristic of a new formulation of the demand Foucault states: "The demand can now be articulated in terms of a potentiality, a future that is immediate, which is already present in the present because it concerns a certain function of Statist universality that is already fulfilled by 'a' nation within the social body, and which is therefore demanding that its status as a single nation must be effectively recognised, and recognised in the juridical form of the State." (Foucault 2003 pg. 222). The bourgeois discourse is then demanding a contract arising from its public right rooted in Statist universality. A contract where the hegemony of the bourgeoisie is rooted and assured in its control and dominance of the State. In exchange the other nations, lacking in capacity and capability to unleash Statist universality, will gain access through the actions of the bourgeoisie that unleashes Statist universality on all nations of the social body. The three card hustle where the bourgeoisie is articulating a power relation, not a threat of the unleashing of force to achieve domination. The bourgeoisie wants the other nations to buy into the contract, thereby policing themselves. This power relation demands that the bourgeoisie redefine what constitutes a nation and it is expected that the discourse must posit that its relationship with the State defines a nation, thereby dismissing the history of that nation and especially its relations with other nations. Foucault states: "You see, what, in these conditions, defines a nation is not its archaism, its ancestral nature, or its relationship with the past; it is its relationship with something else, with the State." (Foucault 2003 pg. 223). The State must define the nation in order for the strategic primacy of the bourgeoisie to be established, hence its public right to contractual acceptance and acquiescence by the other nations devoid of the ability to generate progress. The discursive agents of the bourgeoisie having already formulated the strategic end are now reverse engineering the mechanism and its apparatuses of power to attain this strategic end. This is a most potent insight into why discourse has to be tactically polyvalent. This bourgeois discourse is in fact a mechanism of power that expands into a discourse by absorbing a range of discursive constructs from various discourses as: law, sovereignty and juridical discourse, public right, a nation, the noble savage and the contract, *Homo economicus* and race, nationalism, racism and white supremacy and most of all the problematization of difference. This polyglot Tower of Babel is erected to establish the public right of the bourgeoisie to rule by contract. Foucault continues on the bourgeois nation as follows: "its ability to administer itself, to manage, govern, and guarantee the constitution and workings of the figure of the State and State power. Not domination but State control." "The nation is the active, constituent core of the State. The nation is the State, or at least an outline State." (Foucault 2003 pg. 223). The bourgeois nation, through its unique talents in self-management and self-control, is the only nation that can constitute the State. The State is then the expression of the existential condition and reality of the bourgeois nation. A position riddled with racist arrogance and bourgeois supremacy which feeds the construct of white supremacy within bourgeois discourse. But it is noteworthy that bourgeois discourse is insisting that it does not promote, nor is driven by the construct of bourgeois domination nor State domination as the State and the bourgeoisie are not a single entity. The State wields control over the totality of the social order as its universalist nature precludes domination and constitutes a specificity of nature and operationalisation that is distinct, separate and apart from the bourgeois nation. This is a discourse of truth propagated by bourgeois discourse to bolster the effectiveness of the construct of human rights and the rule of law which must constantly mask the power/force relations that drive the relationship between bourgeoisie and the State and the bourgeoisie and the other nations in the social order.

Bourgeois Dialecticised Historical Knowledge

The bourgeoisie is then writing a specific history of the State entirely distinct from the position adopted by the discourse of race war. On this new bourgeois discourse of history Foucault states: "We now have a discourse on history that is more sympathetic to the State and which is no longer, in its essential functions, anti-State. The objective of this new history is not, however, to let the State speak its own self-justificatory discourse. It is to write the history of the relations that are forever being woven between nation and State, between the nation's Statist potential and the actual totality of the State." (Foucault 2003 pg. 224). This is a history written in praise of the unique qualities of the bourgeoisie which results in the unique potential of the bourgeoisie to be the social force that brings into being the universality of the Statist totality. This is a bourgeois centred history with its gaze fixed on the State, but only articulating the imminent greatness of the bourgeoisie. In this history the universalist State is the voiceless hostage of the bourgeois artifice of pointing to the State, whilst the State is voiceless and the bourgeoisie speaks for the State being the Oracle of the Statist totality. Foucault continues: "This, therefore, is a history that is polarised toward the present and toward the State, a history that culminates in the immanence of the State, of the total, complete, and full figure of the State in the present. And this will also make it possible-second point-to write a history in which the relations of force that are in play are not of a warlike nature, but completely civilian, so to speak." (Foucault 2003 pgs.224-225). This is a discourse of history of the present where the sleight of hand is the immanence of the State in its universalist totality which begets into operational existence the construct of force relations that are not driven by domination, for we are all endowed with human rights under the rule of law. This sleight of hand is a device to distract from the reality of power/force relations and the hegemony of the bourgeoisie, which falsifies the discourse of human rights under the rule of law. Foucault continues: "We now have, in contrast, a history in which war-the war for domination-will be replaced by a struggle that is, so to speak, of a different substance: not an armed clash, but an effort, a rivalry, a striving for the universality of the State." (Foucault 2003 pg. 225). Under the totality generated by the universality of the State there is no war for domination as the force relations of the totality have changed fundamentally as they are now rivalries premised on the actions to ensure and promote the universality of the State. The totality is then organic and all members of the totality are constituted by and serve the hegemony of the universality of the State. Simply gobblygook posing as a discourse of truth seeking to mask the operational reality of power relations. Foucault continues: "The State, and the universality of the State, become both what is at stake in the struggle, and the battlefield. This will therefore be an essentially civil struggle to the extent that domination is neither its goal or nor its expression, and to the extent that the State is both its object and its space. It will take place essentially in and around the economy, institutions, production, and the administration. We will have a civil struggle, and the military struggle or bloody struggle will become no more than an exceptional moment, a crisis or an episode within it." (Foucault 2003 pg. 225). Within the ambit of the totality conjured up by the universality of the State there is then no domination, no force relations, no power relations premised on interpersonal contestations within shared spaces generated by an immense range of reasons for contestations. In this discourse of truth/denial all possible spaces of contestation are now summed up in the State, therefore the State is the contested space and the reason for the contested space. Hence the reason why the struggle is not over domination for the god of the totality cannot be dominated by its subjects nor allow itself to dominate as it is a universality. All struggle will then be civil, located in the expressions of the totality as its institutions ensuring that war, military engagement will become necessary solely as a result of crisis, but its necessity still exists. In its quest to create a historical discourse that banishes domination, violence and war as being endemic to the social order the future replaces the present with the universality of the State, which unleashes the totality of the State that constitutes the social order. The metaphysical, mythic entity formulated the universality of the State then brings it all into existence in the eye of the discursive agents, but there is a dire need for a mechanism of power with its apparatuses on the ground. Enter the mechanism of power of biopolitics with its attendant race supremacist apparatuses, which are an operational contradiction to the construct of the universality of the State. The bourgeois discourse creates a new historical intelligibility that enables the formulation and operationalisation of biopolitics. Foucault states: "And now we have a very different grid of historical intelligibility. Once history is polarised around the nation/State, virtuality/ actuality, functional totality of the nation/real universality of the State, you can see clearly that the present becomes the fullest moment, the moment of the greatest intensity, the solemn moment when the universal makes it entry into the real." (Foucault 2003 pg. 227). The present is then only The Present when the universality of the State is revealed at a specific moment. The Present is only the present when there is the moment of revelation. Without this moment of revelation, the present is the state of mindlessness, of slumber, of the futureless present where there is domination, war and bloodletting. The basic form of the construct is a duality rooted in key dualities that are locked in an operational dance or the dialectic. This dialectic is rooted in the duality virtuality/actuality where the moment of revelation makes the virtual adopt an actual state of operational existence that is only possible because of the operational existence of the bourgeoisie. This is the overarching discursive construct that drives the conception of a minority group within the social order as being the essence of progress in the historical tradition of the Judeo-Christian discourse of the prophets of God. This construct has then an apocalyptic worldview that is hidden but yet insinuated by its dualist structure, for all dualities are gravely intolerant of difference and resistance. It labours under the burden of a construct of uniqueness that denotes fitness to rule and intolerance of opposition to its rule where difference will express backwardness, unfitness to rule and unfitness to live, hence the need for the Final Solution. It is a construct that seeks the same ends as those of the monarchists and the nobility, but via a new construct that will create "science" as the means to prove fitness/unfitness to rule and ensure efficient and cost effective termination of threats posed. This construct can only visualise and formulate in dualities, where time is a straight line and nothing is cyclical. Their premier scientist was Newton.

Dual Grids of Intelligibility

Foucault is then positing two histories: one driven by domination and the other by the totality interacting with, rubbing up against each other in a contestation for hegemony. But in the flow of discursive contestation there must be cross fertilisation arising from the human capacity to traverse the terrain of discourses in contestation. This arises from Foucault's position that each discourse is a grid of intelligibility, which it must be in order to constitute humans as objects of knowledge. Foucault states: "A history that is written, then, both in terms of an initial rift and a totalising completion. And I think that the utility, the political utilisability, of historical discourse is basically defined by the interplay between these two grids, or by the way in which one or the other of them is privileged." (Foucault 2003 pg. 228). For Foucault the political utility of both historical discourses is directly connected to their performance in the contestations with each other, which is understood. To attain hegemony means being a privileged discourse, thereby the highest state of political utilisability. But hegemony and political utilisability ultimately hinges on the intelligibility, the understandability of the discourse. Foucault states: "Broadly speaking, if the first grid of intelligibility-the initial rift-is privileged, the result will be a history that can, if you like, be described as reactionary, aristocratic, and rightist. If the second-the present moment of universality-is privileged, we will have a history of the liberal or the bourgeois type." (Foucault 2003 pg. 2228). The discourse is the grid of intelligibility and in a position of dominance/privilege this intelligibility generates the summation of its constructs into a typology spectrum: rightist to liberal, aristocratic/reactionary to bourgeois/liberal. But the typology is in itself the product of hegemony/privilege an expression of, an instrument of, and the product of power relations. Foucault continues: "But neither of these histories, each of which has its own tactical position, can actually avoid having to use both grids in one way or another." (Foucault 2003 pg. 228). The contestation of two or more grids of intelligibility demands the accessibility of all grids to each other as it is a tactical imperative. What this then enables is the expansion of the constructs of the discourses in engagement towards attaining dominance, but what it produces are in fact discourses with extensions/apparatuses of power which are in fact in contradiction to the public message of the discourse. The graver the contestation the more the process of hybridisations intensifies, which can reach the point where the internal terrain of the discourse is reformulated in noted contradiction to its public message. This is particularly noted in political discourses of the North Atlantic in the 21st century.

Bourgeois Dialectic History and Philosophy

Foucault in the closing statements of the session now turns to the development of a philosophy of history that matches the bourgeois discourse of history in its rejection of war and domination in the analysis of the social order; and in the specificity of this discourse the dialectic is formulated. Historical discourse was not dialecticised through the importation of a philosophy of history imbued with the dialectic. Rather the discourse of history self-dialecticised via the changes made by the bourgeoisie to the historical discourse of the eighteenth century, making possible the formulation of a philosophy of history rooted in the dialectic in the nineteenth century. Foucault states: "What took place was a self-dialecticalisation of historical discourse, and it occurred independently of any explicit transposition-or any explicit utilisation-of a dialectical philosophy into a historical discourse." (Foucault 2003 pgs. 238-237). The discursive constructs of the present, the universality of the State and the uniqueness of the bourgeoisie were then the basis of the formulation of the dialectic, which then self-dialecticised the discourse as it flexed its discursive muscles in its engagement with contending discourses. Foucault states: "From the nineteenth century onward something new-and, I think, something fundamental-began to happen. History and philosophy began to ask the same questions: What is it, in the present, that is the agent of the universal? What is it, in the present, that is the truth of the universal? That is the question asked by history. It is also the question asked by philosophy. The dialectic is born." (Foucault 2003 pg. 237). The questions of the nature of the truth of and the agent of the universal in the present, not the past nor the future, but in the here and now, constitute the dialectic which drives in the nineteenth century a discourse of history and a philosophy of history rooted in the dialectic. The bourgeoisie has then formulated two discourses of the dialectic in the nineteenth century that is their assault vehicle in the quest for hegemony over the social order. The very said dialectic that Karl Marx and Friedrich Engels adopted, and supposedly reconfigured, where the proletariat was now the truth and the agent of the universal in the present dominated by the bourgeoisie. A dialectic in which the agent of the universal will destroy bourgeois hegemony by dint of the dialectical forces operationalised in the mode of production and publicly expressed via class struggle. All that was required was the physical existence of the agent of the universal and the truth of the universal was understood, thereby obviating the need for the agent of the universal to consciously operationalise itself and discourse towards the event. The relations of production will inevitably push the proletariat along the path necessary to reveal the truth of the agent of the universal in the present. In this dialectic the agent of the universal is located in a totality where the universal limits the agency of the subjects of the totality, for the truth of the universal and its revelation cannot be limited by human consciousness and agency. The Marx and Engels dialectic then creates a jealous universal that polices the truth of and the agents of the universal through a totality that problematizes resistance and difference as infections of the totality that must be stamped out. The mechanism and apparatuses of power utilised by this dialectic to purge the threats to the totality are all borrowed from the bourgeois discourse of history this discourse of historical materialism was drawn from. This is potently indicated by the racism common to Marx and Lenin in their writings on the people of Asia and Africa and their fitness for revolution. Apparently, the truth of and the agent of the universal in the present was the exclusive domain of white European people, especially for Marx and Lenin. Foucault's position on the dialectic marked the end of the penultimate session ten of the public lecture of 1976.

Chapter Eight
Session Eleven: 17 March 1976
Power, Racism and State Racism

In session ten Foucault dealt with the disappearance of war from historical analysis, now at the commencement of session eleven he indicates that he will deal with State racism which absorbed the construct of race. Foucault states that the construct of race was absorbed, but not entirely deactivated or obliterated from European discourse. State racism is inextricably tied to power's hold over life, where in the nineteenth century power over man the living being entailed State control over the biological reality of man the living being. In the nineteenth century the focus shifted to understanding and constituting knowledges/disciplines of the biology of man towards State control of the biological processes of man. Foucault commences at the point of the reformulation of the concept of the right of sovereignty where the old hegemonic right to take life or let live was complemented, penetrated but not supplanted by a new right to make live and let die. This new right can only be exercised via control over the biological processes of birth and death under State control. Population control exercised via the medicalisation of the population. Medical discourse and its mechanism and apparatuses of power are core strategic instruments of State control of the biology of man the living being. Foucault states: "The right of sovereignty was the right to take life or let live. And then the new right is established: the right to make live and to let die." (Foucault 2003 pg. 241). But in his analysis of the emergence of this new right Foucault focuses not on political theory, but on the nature of power and its evolution. Foucault states: "I would in fact like to trace the transformation not at the level of political theory, but rather at the level of the mechanisms, techniques, and technologies of power." (Foucault 2003 pg. 241).

State Racism and Biopower

Foucault states that in the seventeenth and eighteenth centuries techniques of power appeared which focused on the human body, specifically on the individual human body which was individualised, surveilled and disciplined strictly in the domain of labour and the efficiency of labour. This was then a disciplinary technology of labour at the heart of the capitalist factory order: docile, surveilled, cheap, available, politically neutered labour. The new right will then emerge from a new technique of power, which is not a disciplinary technology, but it does not dissolve the disciplinary technology of labour, in fact in the late 20th century and the early 21st century this disciplinary technology of labour is globalised under the hegemony of neoliberalism. The new nondisciplinary power is applied to man the living being, to man-as-species in an attempt to exert control over the species; unlike the disciplinary technology of labour and other disciplinary technologies, which attempt to control the mass of humans by turning them into individuals who are then disciplined as they police themselves within the social order. Foucault states: "So after the first seizure of power over the body in an individualising mode, we have a second seizure of power that is not individualising but, if you like, massifying, that is directed not at man-as-body but man-as-species. After the anatomo-politics of the human body established in the course of the eighteenth century, we have, at the end of that century, the emergence of something that is no longer an anatomo-politics of the human body, but what I would call a 'biopolitics' of the human race." (Foucault 2003 pg. 243). This non anatomo-politics of the human race or biopolitics is then the technology of power that constitutes State racism. State racism is the discourse that then produces disciplinarianised knowledges into disciplines of scientific racism, as eugenics and social Darwinism, and launches the discipline of white supremacy with their attendant political discourses. The disciplinary technology of labour and other disciplinary technologies march in lockstep with biopolitics creating a diverse, fluid, interlocked and intense terrain of power relations in the social order. White supremacy is one such disciplinary technology utilised to police non-whites in the social order, while it constitutes the acceptable non-white individual and the acceptable white individual. For the process utilised we must turn to Frantz Fanon. For Foucault in the second half of the eighteenth century the first objects of knowledge of biopolitics were the birth rate, the mortality rate and the life span of the human, which gave birth to the discipline of demography and they all impacted the evolution of medical knowledge.

Medical knowledge now focuses on public hygiene which inevitably is rooted in State control. Biopolitics is in fact expressed via State control and growing State power and intervention into the daily lives of the human race, which attaches its operational focus on the individual members of the human race comprising the social order from conception to death. In the operational realm of biopolitics there is a fixation with mortality, hence an entirely different approach to and definition of death, for death is now a grave threat. In effect this is a symptom of the medicalisation of the population that is demanded by the techniques of power of biopolitics. Foucault states: "Death was no longer something that suddenly swooped down on life-as in an epidemic. Death was now something permanent, something that slips into life, perpetually gnaws at it, diminishes it and weakens it." (Foucault 2003 pg. 244). In listing the domains of biopolitics in the late eighteenth and early nineteenth centuries Foucault ends the list with the domain of the relations between the human race, human beings and the milieu, the environment in which they live, specifically the urban environment/milieu. Biopolitics of the first incarnation is then amongst other domains intent on impacting the relationship between the human race and the designation and forming of space into a human environment/milieu. Biopolitics is then from its first incarnation a deeply political order which affixes the gaze not on the individual, but the human race. And in the terrain of this macro gaze space is afforded racist discourse as a strategic instrument of differentiation of the masses of humanity into designated groupings, which enable the application of instruments of regularisation. Foucault states: "What we are dealing with in this new technology of power is not exactly society..., nor is it the individual-as-body. It is a new body, a multiple body, a body with so many heads that, while they may not be infinite in number, cannot necessarily be counted." (Foucault 2003 pg. 245). The focus of biopolitics is the biological body with multiple heads, persons, personalities and behaviours. Biopolitics is then the combination of problems which biology and politics pose at the level of the human race and the technology of power to contain them. Foucault states: "Biopolitics deals with the population, with the population as political problem, as a problem that is at once scientific and political, as a biological problem and as power's problem." (Foucault 2003 pg. 245). But the phenomena generated by the approach to population as multifaceted, multiple problems are aleatory serial events which demand a technology of power that is nondisciplinary. The challenge then is what is the technology of power formulated to deal with aleatory serial events that play out over time? Foucault states: "The phenomena addressed by biopolitics are essentially, aleatory events that occur within a population that exists over a period of time." (Foucault 2003 pg. 246). These aleatory events within a population have to be impacted in order to produce an equilibrium or to maintain an average. A regulatory technology of power is then necessary, not a disciplinary technology of power, as they are entirely different in formulation and focus. Both technologies of power maximise and extract forces, but a regulatory technology of power acts upon the population, the collective of humans unlike a disciplinary power, that solely focuses on the individual body. The regulatory technology of power is solely concerned with creating an equilibrium, a regularity of the biological processes, of taking of control of life by having regularised the biological processes of man-as-species not disciplined. Biopolitics is State racism as hegemonic State discourse determines what biological processes of man-as-species present grave threats to the social order, which are then the focus of regularisation by the technology of power of regularisation. Biopolitics/State racism problematizes difference in the realm of biology, thereby bringing into the list of possible choices of regularisation strategies the following: *eugenics, Gulag, Dachau, apartheid, Jim Crow legislation and the Final Solution*. Foucault states: "There is absolutely no question relating to an individual body, in the way that discipline does. It is therefore not a matter of taking the individual at the level of individuality but, on the contrary, of using overall mechanisms and acting in such a way to achieve overall states of equilibration or regularity; it is, in a word, a matter of taking control of life and the biological processes of man-as-species and of ensuring that they are not disciplined, but regularised." (Foucault 2003 pgs. 246-247).

The Power of Regularisation

Regularisation is then the application of a technology of power to life to bend life and its underlying biological processes to fit a mould, a contrived reality that is the basis of *equilibrium* as defined by a hegemonic discourse. And of course there is no assurance that this contrived reality in fact flows with the intrinsic operational reality of the biological processes. Regularisation is then the application of power to biological processes in the quest for human hegemony over the biology of man-the-species. Specifically, of white, males of a specific class position exerting hegemony over the biology of man-the-species. With sustainable hegemony there is then *equilibrium,* but there is blow back from the quest for *equilibrium* which mounts an ever increasing potent threat to *equilibrium.* Foucault states: "It is continuous, scientific, and it is the power to make live. Sovereignty took life and let live. And now we have the emergence of a power that I would call the power of regularisation, and it, in contrast, consists in making live and letting die." (Foucault 2003 pg. 247). There are two entirely different technologies of power now in operation, whereas the old sovereignty wielded the power to take life and to not take life through its claim to the monopoly on violence in the social order; regularisation invests in hegemony over biological processes bound up with death, therefore by its action and inaction it makes live by putting off death and allows to die by *not* postponing death. This reality is illustrated via the medium of public hygiene, public health and death rates. The technology of power of regularisation is then focused on mortality not death, for death is inevitable driven by a medicalising discourse. Death then is outside of the grip of or the expanse of power which makes it a viable instrument of power as it enables the formulation and operationalisation of the Final Solution, whilst inhabiting a realm reserved for realities marginalised by power. Death can then be unleashed as an instrument of power in search of *equilibrium* in a cocoon of denial, lies and rationalisations. Foucault states: "Death is outside the power relationship. Death is beyond the reach of power, and power has a grip on it only in general, overall, or statistical terms. Power has no control over death, but it can control mortality." "Power no longer recognises death. Power literally ignores death." (Foucault 2003 pg. 248). This *equilibrium* sought through the application of a specific technology of power must ignore death whilst it focuses on mortality, but for what purpose and what reason? Foucault states: "This is a technology which aims to establish a sort of homeostasis, not by training individuals, but by achieving an overall equilibrium that protects the security of the whole from internal dangers." (Foucault 2003 pg. 249). The technology of power is formulated and operationalised to deal with internal threats to security generated by the life processes of man-the-species, there are then biological threats posed by man-the-species to man-the-species contained within a social order with an order of power. The question then is how do you operationalise a technology of power against the biological processes of man-the-species?

The Norm and the Normalising Society

Foucault returns to the operational nature of two technologies of power in the social order that are structurally different yet operationally are not mutually exclusive as there exist realities of the human condition in a social order where they both impact, such as sexuality. Foucault states: "Both technologies are obviously technologies of the body, but one is a technology in which the body is individualised as an organism endowed with capacities, while the other is a technology in which bodies are replaced by general biological processes." (Foucault 2003 pg. 249). One technology constitutes the individualised, capacity laden body held together in the matrix bonded by the construct of self which polices itself. The other deals with general biological processes that generate threats to the order of power. Two distinct technologies: one technology constitutes the individualised body, the self, the person, the desiring individual with capacities and agency and the other technology constitutes the body as the expression of and terrain of biological processes. Two distinct technologies constitituting two distinct bodies but for strategic reasons cannot be mutually exclusive, as there must be an operational boundary between them that is specific yet fluid, interchangeable yet distinct, which presents then a grave challenge to the hegemony of power as it constitutes the ever fluid never static terrain of power relations which demands that power be ever strategic in its intent. Foucault continues: "So we have two series: the body organism-discipline-institutions series, and the population-biological processes-regulatory mechanisms-State. An organic-institutional set, or the organo-discipline of the institution, if you like, and, on the other hand, a biological and Statist, or bioregulation by the State." (Foucault 2003 pg. 250). The terminal point of the disciplinary technology is the institutions of the technology, whilst the other given its operational nature its terminal point must be the State. But this distinction between State and institutions does not impute a dichotomy between them as the space between them in this disciplinary technology is an operational necessity, not the existence of a space in which the State is excluded from. What is much more significant is the fact that both technologies are not mutually exclusive as they operate in entirely different strategic terrains. Which means that they operate in tandem on targeted bodies, as is the case of sexuality. Foucault states: "sexuality represents the precise point where the disciplinary and the regulatory, the body and the population are represented." (Foucault 2003 pg. 252). In the operational state of both technologies in sexuality the State must then be involved in the operations of both technologies of power. Operational challenges as sexuality then demand a power/knowledge that addresses the operational complexities of both technologies simultaneously, which in the case of sexuality is medicine power/knowledge. The both operational technologies are also applied to abnormal behaviour and abnormal persons, which include deviants as the criminogenic etc., with the relevant power/knowledge formulated and applied as psychiatry, criminology, psychotherapy etc. Foucault states: "Medicine is a power-knowledge that can be applied to both the body and the population, both the organism and biological processes, and it will therefore have both disciplinary effects and regulatory effects." (Foucault 2003 pg. 252). The regulatory technology of power seized and ensured that the discourse of medicine in the nineteenth century evolved the requisite knowledge/power apparatuses to address the need to regulate the biological processes of man-the-species. In addition to its power/knowledge apparatuses necessary to the disciplinary technology of the body where both technologies operationally overlap, impact and cross-fertilise each other. In this operational scenario there must be an operational element that applies to both technologies of power which affords control of the operations of both technologies. This element has to be applicable operationally simultaneously to the body that has to be disciplined and the population that has to be regularised. Foucault defines this element as the "norm", which is the basis of the order of the normalising society. For Foucault the normalising society is not the product of a generalised disciplinary order that has consumed the society. A normalising society can only be the product of the disciplinary and the regulatory technologies where they intersect, as in sexuality. This is an intersection of the specific norm of each technology of power. Foucault states: "The normalising society is a society in which the norm of discipline and the norm of regulation intersect along an orthogonal articulation." (Foucault 2003 pg. 253). External of the point of intersection of both norms they are distinct, separate and apart from each other, except at the point of intersection where they share and cover a common space. The basis of normalisation is the common space shared at the point of intersection, where that space and all therein is normalised. In the domain of sexuality normalised sexuality is all that is contained at the point of intersection of the two norms of power. All that lies between the organic and the biological, between the body and population is the terrain of the intersections of the two norms of the technologies of power, hence normalised. Foucault in this final session does not grapple with the identity of the entity that constitutes the two norms, fails to show how normalisation is expressed politically in the social order and finally state the purpose behind normalisation and the interests it serves. What he does say is that eventually biopolitics surpasses the power of sovereign right and it is progressively relegated as biopolitics enables man to manage life and ultimately destroy all life and the planet that houses that life. Foucault is stating that biopower/biopolitics is beyond all human sovereignty, which again raises the issue of the identity of the discourse that exerts hegemony over biopolitics and its nature. Does this overlord discourse then wield a technology of power that enables control and direction to biopower?

Biopower and Racist Normative Space

At this juncture in the session Foucault now addresses the salient construct of his public lecture 1976. Foucault posits the question which asks how will biopower, through its two technologies of power that makes life its object and objective, how will the power to kill and to murder operate in biopower? Under the sovereignty of right, the State insisted on its monopoly of violence, its right to kill, to murder. How does a State rooted in the two norms of the technologies of power of biopower murder, kill and take life? Can it kill if it stays in line with its discourse? This is Foucault's mind games, for under the hegemony of biopolitics there were two World Wars in the twentieth century that broke out in Europe and prosecuted on a world scale. These World Wars illustrate the reality that biopower/biopolitics has no aversion, and can in fact murder on an industrial scale with industrial efficiency and rationality. Foucault states: "how will the power to kill and the function of murder operate in this technology of power, which takes life as both its object and its objective?" "Given that this power's objective is to essentially make live, how can it let die? How can the power of death, the function of death, be exercised in a political system centered upon biopower?" (Foucault 2003 pg. 254). Biopower/biopolitics and the State it constitutes must kill efficiently, but how do you operationalise killing as a biological process where biological threats are identified and terminated for the good of the social order? What then is the apparatus of power through which you gaze upon the biological landscape creating classifications/typologies of dualities: the wanted /unwanted, the normal/abnormal, the good/evil, other, the accepted/the threat? Foucault insists that this instrument is racism in all its forms. These typologies of dualities then constitute the threat horizon and demand that the social order must be defended by any means necessary. Foucault states: "It is indeed the emergence of this biopower that inscribes it in the mechanisms of the State. It is at this moment that racism is inscribed as the basic mechanism of power, as it is exercised in modern States. As a result, the modern State can scarcely function without becoming involved with racism at some point, within certain limits and subject to certain conditions." (Foucault 2003 pg. 254). Biopower/ biopolitics finds racism, with its long history in European societies, absorbs and reformulates it as a mechanism of power, which means that all power relations in the North Atlantic are the operational terrain of the mechanism of racism. These social orders are then functionally racist social orders. Racism is organic to their worldview and the go to mechanism to deal with difference – an automatic, conditioned knee jerk reaction, even instinctual. Foucault defines racism as follows: "It is primarily a way of introducing a break into the domain of life that is under power's control: the break between what must live and what must die." (Foucault 2003 pg. 254). The diversity of the human race, potently illustrated by the diversity of races and mixtures of races, is the premier terrain where the mechanism of power of racism is applied to create typologies. Foucault states: "the hierarchy of races, the fact that certain races are described as good and the others are described as inferior: all this is a way of fragmenting the field of the biological that power controls." (Foucault 2003 pg. 255). Being a mechanism of power racism has functions allocated to it by biopower, one of which is to subdivide the human race/the species into subdivisions of races where typologies and a hierarchy of races enable biopower to exert power on the biological processes of these races. What is also apparent is that disciplinary power also utilises the artifices of the mechanism of biopower, i.e. racism, by which to discipline the bodies of those in these categories. This mechanism of biopower, a regulatory power, enables the operationalisation of disciplinary power and both of them operate through different racist norms which intersect and create racist normative space which eventually captures and wields political power. Racist normative space then extols the political discourse of white supremacy/white power. This racist normative space was given new life with the War on Terror commencing in 2001, where an inferior race with their inferior discourse was now portrayed by hegemonic North Atlantic discourse as presenting a grave threat to the world hegemon of the post-World Wars era. Politicians traversed the racist normative space in a bid to ensure their political sustainability setting the tone for the response of the social order. The manner in which the War on Terror was and is prosecuted to this day illustrates the reality that the overt and covert agencies of the state are now driven by the mechanism of power of the racist normative space, with Guantanamo Bay being its shining symbol.

Foucault presents the functions of racism to biopower as follows: "That is the first function of racism, to fragment, to create caesuras within the biological continuum addressed by biopower." (Foucault 2003 pg. 255). This then is racism as an instrument of biopower, not racism as an instrument of the sovereignty of right and the disciplinary technology of the body. This is racism expressed as a racist hierarchy that impacts the DNA of man-the-species. This is eugenics that is now concerned with genetic manipulation to ensure the hegemony of biopower and its race hierarchy. For biopower, race and the race hierarchy is palpably real making the typology of 'ethnicity' a vassal, subservient discourse of truth. The second function of racism is as follows according to Foucault: "Racism also has a second function. Its role is, if you like, to allow the establishment of a positive function of this type: 'The more you kill, the more death you will cause' or 'The very fact that you let more die will allow you to live more.'" (Foucault 2003 pg. 255). Racism places on the agenda of biopower the necessity to cull the herd for killing impacts mortality, it exerts power over mortality whilst it expunges the less than perfect, the abnormal, the inferior and the infirm from the herd. The old lessons racism learnt from its operations under the sovereignty of right and the disciplinary technology of the body it imports into the regulatory technology of the species and impacts this technology of biopower and man-the-species in a dramatic, even revolutionary fashion. Foucault continues: "But racism does make the relationship of war- 'If you want to live, the other must die'-function in a way that is completely new and that is quite compatible with the exercise of biopower." (Foucault 2003 pg. 255). Over time racism in the North Atlantic has evolved and the racism of massa on the plantation cannot provide instruments by which to dismantle the racism of biopower. Foucault sums up the two functions of racism in the service of biopower as follows: "On the one hand, racism makes it possible to establish a relationship between my life and the death of the other that is not a military or warlike relationship of confrontation, but a biological-type relationship." (Foucault 2003 pg. 255). The biological demands of man-the-species make it mandatory that the herd be culled, which is not a war of conquest or genocide, but an act of killing that is vitally necessary to ensure that the species is purer and as a result healthier. The Final Solution was then biologically necessary, seen in the fact that those who defeated Nazi Germany of the North Atlantic possess a long history of purging elements defined as the inferior, the abnormal and the criminogenic, such as the Native Populations and the African enslaved. Racism as an instrument of the regulatory mechanism of power is operating strictly within the bounds of a biological process, not warlike, military or political relationships, but it soon impacts the military, the order of war and political relationships seen in the conjunctures the two World Wars were in the history of man-the-species and thereafter. This was and is so because biopower utilising racism as its angel of death fundamentally changed the nature of the North Atlantic State. It became a State where killing and murder by the State became purely biologically determined processes for the greater good of humanity, as illustrated by the two World Wars and thereafter. Foucault states: "Once the State functions in the biopower mode, racism alone can justify the murderous function of the State." (Foucault 2003 pg. 256). A State under the hegemony of biopower can then only be a racist State, which will relentlessly prove repeatedly that democracy is a discourse of truth in the service of biopower. Officer, Officer/Overseer, Overseer. And every vestige of a technology of power seeking operational status in the order of biopower must be racist, for it is only through racism that they can communicate with the technology of normalisation of biopower. In the State constituted by biopower racism is the language of the technologies of power as they communicate with the technology of normalisation. They will simply fail to be operationalised in a biopower State without being able to communicate with the technology of normalisation and to do this they must utilise racism. The point of communication is where non-biopower constructs of racism that span the gamut of North Atlantic racist discourse enter into the discursive flow and impact the racism of biopower, especially in the realm of politics and political mobilisation. Foucault states: "If the power of normalisation wished to exercise the old sovereign right to kill, it must become racist. And if, conversely, a power of sovereignty, or in other words, a power that has the right to life and death, wishes to work with the instruments, mechanisms, and technology of normalisation, it too must become racist." (Foucault 2003 pg. 256). The disciplinary technology of the body and the regulatory technology of life each possess and operationalise racist norms, which ensure that normalised space is racist in the entirety of North Atlantic racist discourse or the abode of white supremacist discourse. Biopolitics, racism and State racism are located in the man-as-species space and expressed as biological/genetic imperatives in that medium, but when biopolitics, race and State racism enter the medium of politics they are expressed as war emerging from a biological medium; where threats posed to the superior race by the inferior races necessitate war to eliminate the threat, thereby plumbing the depths of the discourse of race war once again. This is potently indicated by the embrace of evolutionism and its manner of political expression.

Biopower and Evolutionism

Nineteenth century biological theory was rapidly absorbed by the discourse of power, where evolutionism became a discourse in its own right in the service of biopower. The discourse of evolutionism was then the application of racism to a discourse rooted in a biological interpretation of reality and the solutions derived thereof. Foucault states on evolutionism: "but a real way of thinking about the relations between colonisation, the necessity of wars, criminality, the phenomena of madness and mental illness, the history of societies with their different classes, and so on." (Foucault 2003 pg. 257). The discourse of evolutionism was the grid through which reality involving conquest, domination, extermination and the protection of society was constituted, sifted and solutions devised. The discourse of evolutionism therefore justified domination and extermination, just simply killing.

The base reality is that racism was embraced by biopower and the modern European State and racism became openly expressed and utilised in the social order of these States at times when the taking of life was imperative, as in wars of imperial conquest. And in the War on Terror in the 21st century the biopolitics of States of the North Atlantic are again exhibiting the expression of racism in the political domain. This recurring public wave of racist engagement is the product of the use of racism, combined with evolutionism, to justify the need to kill, to defang all threats posed. But various constructs of racism are expressed in the public domain in conjunction with, under the ambit of and under the hegemony of biopolitics, which leads to the falsified position that operational racism in the North Atlantic remains moored to its colonial origins. Which is a position that denies the existence of racist evolutionism in the service of biopolitics at the level of life, of man-the-species.

Biopolitics, Racism and War

Racism and biopolitics will constitute a brand new conception of war in the nineteenth century. Biopolitics will view war as a biological necessity to man-the-species as it eliminates the enemy race thereby improving the superior race, and by culling the herd of the superior race it regenerates the superior race by increasing its purity. Biopolitics then has a blood lust for the good and perfection of the race and the social order. Foucault states: "At the end of the nineteenth century, we have then a new racism modelled on war." (Foucault 2003 pg. 258). From 2001, especially in the USA and the rest of the North Atlantic, the new racism modelled on war is prosecuting an external racist War on Terror and simultaneously an internal racist war against all the threats posed by internal inferior races to the master race. Criminality, madness and various abnormalities were similarly conceptualised in racist terms.

The racism of biopower/biopolitics is then uniquely different from the racism formulated under colonial domination since evolved. Modern racism of the North Atlantic is bound up with the operations of a specific state type: the biopower State, a specific technology of power: biopower and a specific discourse of power/knowledge: biopolitics. Without racism this state type, technology of power and discourse of power will be unfit to attain and exercise hegemony sustainably over social orders of the North Atlantic. With racism, biopower and State racism, the North Atlantic adopted a facsimile of the racist slave states of the colonial empires of Europe. The racist slave states of the Caribbean were the initial experiment that produced the discourse of power and slavery which enabled the absorption and reformulation of racism by biopower in the nineteenth century and thereafter in the North Atlantic. Foucault states: "The specificity of modern racism, or what gives it its specificity, is not bound up with mentalities, ideologies, or the lies of power. It is bound up with the technique of power, with the technology of power. It is bound up with this, and that takes us as far away as possible from the race war and the intelligibility of history. We are dealing with a mechanism that allows biopower to work." (Foucault 2003 pg. 258). For Foucault the old racism had no operational link to a technology of power before biopower. It simply was an instrument that existed in the space afforded it by hegemonic discourse with its attendant technology of power. Biopower/biopolitics changed the landscape where racism operated in dramatically as it now became part of a technology of power and a State form in Europe. But this obtained in the slave states of the Caribbean where power and racism were operationally linked and present in the State form, as it was a racist slave state where racism was expressed and operationalised in African enslavement, where the white master slave owning race was a visible minority race, under the control of the State, both in the Caribbean and in the European metropole. The record of the operational existence of the Caribbean slave states then made it very easy and rapidly possible for biopower to absorb and reformulate racism as its instrument for the justification of its blood lust. Foucault continues: "We are dealing with a mechanism that allows biopower to work. So racism is bound up with the workings of a state that is obliged to use race, the elimination of races, and the purification of the race, to exercise its sovereign power." (Foucault 2003 pg. 258). Biopower in order to be a murderous State, a State driven by the technology of war must then embrace and exercise racism, thereby creating the state form: State racism. And the state driven by biopower can only be a murderous state as it struts out its democratic credentials, which is then a discourse of truth or a lie of power. On this Foucault states: "So you can understand how and why, given these conditions, *the most murderous States are also, of necessity, the most racist.*" (Foucault 2003 pg. 258). For Foucault the most potent example of this was Nazi Germany, but this state is in the 21st century a historical episode, what exists today is the USA. Officer, Officer/ Overseer, Overseer!

Foucault in his presentation on the Nazi State alludes to the extreme form biopower took in its insistence on its right to kill, whereby a trinity of absolute extremism was cobbled together: an absolutely racist State, an absolutely murderous State and an absolutely suicidal State. Foucault then poses the question if all states, all capitalist states under the hegemony of biopower possess the capacity to evolve into the Nazi state form? Foucault states: "The final solution for the other races, and the absolute suicide of the race. This is where the mechanisms inscribed in the workings of the modern State leads. But this play is inscribed in the workings of all States. In all modern States, in all capitalist States? Perhaps not." (Foucault 2003 pgs.260-261). Biopower and State racism inevitably take these States down the path of the Final Solution and suicide of the master race through wars in the name of the good of the master race. That is an organic given. The events of the War on Terror have clearly accelerated the journey of the USA down this path, especially in its political relations. Whilst Europe illustrates its penchant for playing catch up. On the Nazi state Foucault states: "We have, then, in Nazi society something that is really quite extraordinary: this is a society that has generalised biopower in an absolute sense, but which has also generalised the sovereign right to kill. The two mechanisms-...-coincide exactly." (Foucault 2003 pg. 260). What then cemented both mechanisms of power into an organic working whole? It could have only been racism of the Nazi white supremacist nationalist variety. White supremacist nationalist racism then welded together biopower and the old, archaic concept of the right of the State over the life and death of its citizens, thereby creating the trinity of extremism. Foucault states: "The objective of the Nazi regime was not really the destruction of other races. The destruction of other races was one aspect of the project, the other being to expose its own race to the absolute and universal threat of death." (Foucault 2003 pg. 259). The Nazi project was then a success in keeping with its objectives and biopower retains the capacity to this day to replicate the quest for said objectives, for they are organic to biopower.

Foucault insists that biopower/biopolitics is a grand in-depth departure from the discourse of race war and historic intelligibility, which is the outcome of the breach effected by the quest for hegemony of bourgeois discourse. But what must be grasped is the reality that the embrace of racism by biopower is the embrace of a discursive construct whose evolutionary development was placed in overdrive by the discourse of race war. And the constructs of biopower/ biopolitics, with reference to the biological need to kill and to be killed, are logical expansions of and conclusions reached of the constructs of the discourse of race war. Whilst the constructs of the discourse of race war were pinned in a historical time line and medium and biopower/biopolitics reject this, it cannot retract from the continuity of the worldview from the discourse of race war in the seventeenth century to biopower/biopolitics of the nineteenth century and thereafter. The use of race history by the Nazis to pin their State racism to a historical legacy illustrates this continuity; which lives on with the neo-Fascists and neo-Nazis of the North Atlantic in the 21st century.

In the closing stages of the final session of the 1976 public lecture Foucault introduces the construct of social-racism, which was operationalised before the creation of the socialist State in Europe. Social-racism was then a contemporary of biopower and in the nineteenth century social-racism became a construct of socialist discourse from the pre Marxian forms to the Marxian and the Marxian hybrids, as Marxism-Leninism. Foucault is insisting that European socialist discourse from the outset formulated and retained the construct of social-racism. Foucault then insists that the discourse and technology of biopower formulated at the end of the eighteenth and throughout the nineteenth centuries in Europe were embraced and adopted without criticism by socialist theorising during this period. Socialist discourse in fact had an addiction for biopower and the power exercised by the State constituted by racism as a technology of power. Socialism then embraced State racism as the technology of power to enable its State to kill. Foucault insists that this racism was not a truly ethnic racism but an evolutionary, biological racism. In this position Foucault is simply apologetic, for the State termed the Soviet Union exercised both the power of social racism and racist supremacy. To absorb biopower via the fixation on the power of the State of biopower injects racist supremacy into the discourse of socialism, as illustrated by the writings of Marx and Lenin. Foucault states: "Socialism has made no critique of the theme of biopower...it seems to me that socialism takes this over wholesale. And the result is that we immediately find ourselves in a socialist State which must exercise the right to kill or the right to eliminate, or the right to disqualify. And so quite naturally, we find that racism-not a truly ethnic racism, but racism of the evolutionist kind, biological racism-is fully operational in the way socialist States (of the Soviet Union type) deal with the mentally ill, criminals, political adversaries, and so on." (Foucault 2003 pgs. 261-262). The Marxist-Leninist construct that potently illustrates the embrace of the State generated by biopower and racism is the Dictatorship of the Proletariat. The only State form that was capable of operationalising this construct was the State racism of biopower. Foucault states that all forms of socialism in Europe adopted racism as the basis of its technology of power when formulating constructs that dealt with the need and nature of the struggle/battle/war with the agents of capitalism necessary for the overthrow of capitalism. Hence, the uncritical embrace of biopower and State racism which Foucault said destroyed social racism by the end of the nineteenth century with the rise to hegemony of social democracy. Social democracy in fact destroyed the social racism of previous socialisms, as social democracy was the product of and the instrument of biopower and State racism. It is then in the 21st century hilarious to view the call to embrace social democracy as it is the only viable discourse of resistance to austere neoliberal capitalism, where in this discourse there is yet no rejection of biopower. But how can it reject its core construct and its reason for being operationalised? How can the Left attack racist supremacists when they have yet to exorcise biopower and State racism from their discursive constructs?

Foucault ends the 1976 public lecture with a question to all those who speak of change in a social order under the hegemony of biopower. He states: "How can one both make a biopower function and exercise the rights of war, the rights of murder and the function of death, without becoming racist? That was the problem, and that, I think, is still the problem." (Foucault 2003 pg. 263). What then is this change you want? For change with the hegemony of biopower intact is simply business as usual, with a new cosmetic mask applied. Change is then in the 21ˢᵗ century a platitude, a very cruel platitude, that illustrates the hegemony and operational nature of biopower. For all those who speak of racism and racist oppression, yet simultaneously cling tenaciously to biopower, understand you are clinging tenaciously to the very oppression you rant about. You are then simply policing yourself, thereby ensuring and affirming biopower's hegemony over you. The root problem is biopower!

Biopower: History of Sexuality Volume 1: An Introduction

In 1976 "*La Volente de savoir*" was published in France and in 1978 the first American edition in English was published as "The History of Sexuality Volume 1: An Introduction" in which Foucault presented an analysis of biopower with reference to sexuality. In his final two books: "The History of Sexuality Volume 2: The use of pleasure" and "The History of Sexuality Volume 3: The care of the self" Foucault presented no analyses of biopower. In his 1979 public lecture at the College de Paris, though titled "The Birth of Biopolitics", Foucault chose to present on neoliberalism for this public lecture. In his work published in France in 1975 titled "*Surveiller et punir: Naissance et prison*" then in 1977 in English as "Discipline and Punish: The birth of the prison" Foucault dealt with disciplinary techniques of power, not biopower. His oeuvre on biopower is then dominated by the analysis presented in the 1976 public lecture, hence its strategic importance to the study of Foucault's construct of biopower.

In the History of Sexuality Volume 1 Foucault states his genealogy of biopower with reference to sexuality. Foucault commences with the position that wars have changed in Europe as follows: "Wars are no longer waged in the name of a sovereign who must be defended; they are waged on behalf of the existence of everyone; entire populations are mobilised for the purpose of wholesale slaughter in the name of life necessity: massacres have become vital." (Foucault 1990 pg. 137). What has changed the nature of wars and the nature of power wielded that now demands slaughter of life as a life necessity? Foucault continues: "It is as managers of life and survival, of bodies and the race, that so many regimes have been able to wage so many wars, causing so many men to be killed." (Foucault 1990 pg. 137). Power exercised over life, that targets life, that differentiates life as race is what has changed the nature of war in the modern European era. Foucault continues: "If genocide is indeed the dream of modern powers...it is because power is situated and exercised at the level of life, the species, the race, and the large-scale phenomena of population." (Foucault 1990 pg. 137). Power is now being exercised on life, the species and the population of the species differentiated as races, which demands the power to foster life and to forbid it as power defines what is fit and proper life. In the text Foucault posits the example of capital punishment in the modern era, primarily how it becomes redefined and survives under the new era of biopower. To admit to the need to kill a criminal biopower admits its failure to exercise power over the life of the convicted individual and the finality of death ends the ability, potential of power to continue to impact this life. Power had then to redefine capital punishment in its use as an instrument of taking life. Foucault states: "Hence capital punishment could not be maintained except by invoking less the enormity of the crime itself than the monstrosity of the criminal, his incorrigibility, and the safeguard of society. One had the right to kill those who represented a kind of biological danger to others." (Foucault 1990 pg. 138). Danger to life was framed in terms of biological difference that was a threat, hence the embrace of race and racism. This power was now "a power to *foster* life or *disallow* it to the point of death." (Foucault 1990 pg. 138). This new power, as all other power, has a fixation with death as it is the gravest limit to power, illustrated by the fixation with suicide, where the individual chooses death over power, reflected in the formation of the discipline of sociology in the era of this power. Foucault states that suicide "was one of the first astonishments of a society in which political power has assigned itself the task of administering life." (Foucault 1990 pg. 139). The exercise of power over the life of the species, the races and the population was defined by the politics of the social order and the State, which means that political agendas, especially agendas of voter mobilisation and social control, will impact the strategies and emphases of this power over time. The exercise of this power will then be impacted by the rise to hegemony of discourses within the flow of hegemonic discourse. The best examples being the rise to dominance of neoliberalism in the post-world wars in the North Atlantic and its impact on the agenda and strategies of this power and the changing nature of threats and the response of this power to them, such as the Cold War and the War on Terror from 2001.

In describing this power over life Foucault speaks of two forms/poles which in the seventeenth century began the process of branching into two forms. Foucault states: "they constituted rather two poles of development linked together by a whole intermediary cluster of relations." (Foucault 1990 pg. 139). Two distinct poles of human development that exercise power over human life in different spheres, who are not in opposition to each other, but operationalised independently of each other. Yet linked to each other at the intermediary level, not the operational level, for they both exercise power on different aspects of a single human body/life. The first pole that developed was the disciplinary pole of the anatomo-politics of the human body, which views the body as a machine that has to be rendered docile and all its forces and capabilities optimised and harnessed to an economic and political order that ensures the usefulness of the human to that order. The human body has then to be disciplined, where humans police themselves according to the normative order of disciplinary power where they are productive parts of the totality or the whole. Disciplinary power is clearly driven by political agendas and strategies that are driven by the fear of the loss of hegemony. The second pole, which developed after the pole of anatomo-politics of the human body, focuses on the biological processes of life and death of the human species and is operationalised through regulatory controls is a biopolitics of the population. Foucault states: "The disciplines of the body and the regulations of the population constituted the two poles around which the organisation of power over life was deployed. The setting up, in the course of the classical age, of this great bipolar technology-anatomic and biological, individualising and specifying, directed toward the performances of the body, with attention to the processes of life-characterised a power whose highest function was perhaps no longer to kill, but to invest life through and through." (Foucault 1990 pg. 139). A bipolar technology unleashed on all humans of the social order, which is not only two distinct poles not reducible to the condition of each other but two poles that are in effect bipolar as in a duality impacting what is supposedly a single human unit of the species. With resulting bouts of grave and great difference in the power effects sought and effected on the single human of the species.

Foucault maintains that there is bio-power distinct and separate from bio-politics, where bio-power is the sum of the two techniques of power which focus on the human body, whilst bio-politics is the regulatory technology of power. This is a different classification from that of the 1976 public lecture. Foucault's insistence that the two technologies of power were indispensable to the development of capitalism is then the reason for the reformulation of his construct of bio-power, where bio-power outstrips in expanse either one of the two technologies of power. But in this reformulation Foucault has to create an operational context that coordinates both technologies of power in the prosecution of a common strategic end, and for this Foucault locates it in the order of politics. Foucault states: "The adjustment of the accumulation of men to that of capital, the joining of the growth of human groups to the expansion of productive forces and the differential allocation of profit, were made possible in part by the exercise of bio-power in its many forms and modes of application." (Foucault 1990 pg. 141). Foucault continues: "that is the entry of phenomena peculiar to the life of the human species into the order of knowledge and power, into the sphere of political techniques." (Foucault 1990 pgs. 141-142). And: "For the first time in history, no doubt, biological existence was reflected in political existence." (Foucault 1990 pg. 142). The body was then political as there was the politics of the body which was connected to bio-power and the two technologies of power. Foucault continues on the politics of the body and bio-power: "But what might be called a society's 'threshold of modernity' has been reached when the life of the species is wagered on its own political strategies." "modern man is an animal whose politics places his existence as a living being in question." (Foucault 1990 pg. 143). Bio-power, through the operationalisation of its two technologies of power, occupies the realm of politics of the State of the North Atlantic which exposes bio-power to all the power relations of the political order, where bio-power is exposed to the whims and capriciousness of politicians ever mindful of political sustainability. Bio-power navigates the power relations of the State for the State is its vast terminal point as it flows through the social order for it serves the hegemonic order of power and its pool of contending factions in their quest for hegemony, which renders bio-power and the political order that defines its strategies fratricidal. Whilst it carries out its strategic imperative to discipline bodies and regulate the very processes that generate life, take life, preserve life and reproduce life. Bio-power is then bipolar at best, schizoid at worst.

Bio-power begets the normalising society as it needs a dynamic mechanism by which to ensure compliance, discipline and most of all that members of the social order police themselves, for that is the operational environment of power. To accomplish this the norm must be utilised given its flexibility, adaptability and utility, for the norm does not threaten death, but instead seduces the human to comply, to police themselves. The law must then be normalised, it must operate as a norm does, for law and the norm are incompatible. Foucault states: "But a power whose task is to take charge of life needs continuous regulatory and corrective mechanisms...but of distributing the living in the domain of value and utility. Such a power has to qualify, measure, appraise, and hierarchize...it effects distribution around the norm." (Foucault 1990 pg. 144). The primary task of bio-power is formulation and policing of the norm/s which are defined in the cauldron of the power relations of the political order and the State. Bio-power and its norms are then political instruments of power/ knowledge that emanate from the State. This is then the field and expanse of biopolitics on which political mobilisation and political power relations are played out on.

Foucault presents sexuality as the prime example of the targeting of the human body by biopower where sex is a political issue. The pivot of the two axes of biopower, i.e. the disciplinary technology of power and the regulatory technology of biological processes, is the technology of life. The technology of life develops in, inhabits and is operationalised in the pivot of both technologies of power; that normative space formed where both technologies intersect. Foucault states: "it was put forward as the index of a society's strength, revealing of both its political energy and its biological vigour. Spread out from one pole to the other of this technology of sex was a whole series of different tactics that combined in varying proportions the objective of disciplining the body and that of regulating populations." (Foucault 1990 pg.

146). Foucault names four great lines of attack utilised by the politics of sex for over two centuries on the human body. These are: the sexualisation of children, the hysterization of women and their sex were both lines of attack that were demanded by the imperative to regulate biological processes, but a demand for disciplinary control or the policing of oneself was demanded. Disciplinary techniques were then combined with regulatory methods. The other two lines of attack were birth control and the psychiatrisation of perversion, where regulatory methods needed individual disciplines and constraints much more than the first two lines of attack. The four lines of assault on sex resulted in regulatory and disciplining techniques of power requiring the policing of oneself, which was the basis of power relations. Foucault states: "Broadly speaking, at the juncture of the 'body' and the 'population,' sex became a crucial target of a power organised around the management of life rather than the menace of death." (Foucault 1990 pg. 147). Power, power relations and the management of life, not the menace of death, demands that those managed are seduced and buy in to the worldview of hegemonic discourse where they police themselves, obviating the need for the projection of the peril of force or the threat of death. Power's infatuation with sex, the body and life enabled then the embrace of race and racism by power and its technologies of power of the two dominant varieties. Foucault states: "Through the themes of health, progeny, race, the future of the species, the vitality of the social body, power spoke of sexuality and *to* sexuality; the latter was not a mark or a symbol, it was an object and a target." (Foucault 1990 pg. 147). Sexuality was *"an effect with a meaning-value."* (Foucault 1990 pg. 148). Sexuality was an effect of power, but it impacted perceptions, actions and the formulation of discursive constructs in the social order where soon blood, its purity, its potency and its use as a political instrument impacted the analytics of sex, where race, racism, blood, purity and potency now combined within the discourse of sexuality as eugenics. Racism was now an instrument of the technologies of power affixed to sexuality, giving rise to the science of white racist supremacy and its sexuality premised on the sacrosanct nature of blood purity and the master race. Foucault states that in the second half of the nineteenth century the cult of blood was utilised as a political instrument of the political power exercised through the discourse of sexuality. At this juncture scientific, biological racism was formulated and launched as an instrument of biopower. Foucault states: "Racism took shape at this point (racism in its modern, 'biologising,' statist form): it was then a whole politics of settlement (*peuplement*), family, marriage, education, social hierarchizing, and property accompanied by a long series of interventions at the level of the body, conduct, health, and everyday life, received their colour and their justification from the mythical concern with protecting the purity of the blood and ensuring the triumph of the race." (Foucault 1990 pg. 149). Racism, now expressed as the discourse of white supremacy, constituted a social order where space was allocated, the human species was placed in a hierarchy, techniques of power were applied to all individuals of the social order, the political order, the order of power relations and the State, where racism defined the hegemonic worldview and was the binding cement of this matrix. This was then the first organically racist social order in Europe following the slave States of the West Indies.

At the same time of the surge of racism there was the move to reformulate law, sovereignty and the symbolic order in the image and likeness of the discourse of sexuality. The sexual then became reformulated in terms of non biopower constructs, which were co-opted as political instruments to serve biopower. The sexual was then conceived in terms of law, death, blood and sovereignty. Driven by the demands of the politics of biopower in its power relations with the State and the political order, biopower was now absorbing former excluded discourses and reformulating these to operationalise them in the political wars. Biopower was then evolving into a discursive expanse containing various discursive constructs with the capacity to launch bids for hegemony, which can retard the effectiveness of the technologies of power. An assault on the disciplinary technology of power can then result in the breakdown of policing themselves to affirm the hegemony of power. Such an assault on the power relations of sexuality will have the said effect. Foucault states: "On the contrary, sex is the most speculative, most ideal, and most internal element in a deployment of sexuality organised by power in its grip on power and their materiality, their forces, energies, sensations, and pleasures." (Foucault 1990 pg. 155). What then is the impact of the assault of the four lines of attack of power on sex by politics utilising the instrument of law and sovereignty? Politics, law and sovereignty have then changed the operational terrain for the four lines of attack, necessitating reformulation of existing lines and the formulation of new lines. What has been the impact of the technology that separates copulation from reproduction on sex and the lines of attack on sex by power? It is then obvious that instruments of power addressing sexuality have to be continually reformulated in light of push back. For hegemony does not end resistance and resistance begets alternate discourse and technologies of power. How does biopower react to the aging population of the North Atlantic and the economic fallout arising from this specific demographic reality when the politics of the North Atlantic is now averse to, especially non-white, migration? These questions indicate the reality that power is relational, never static, always dynamic and fluid, because power begets resistance. Biopower constantly seeks to absorb subservient discourses and reformulate them in an attempt to keep ahead of the resistance curve. But in this strategy potential diverse constructs develop within hegemonic discourse which can ultimately derail the strategic agenda of biopower. Discursive constructs, predating biopower, can then suddenly spring to life driven by the politics of the State as law, sovereignty and *Homo Economicus*. In the post-World War Two era *Homo Economicus* has attained and exercises hegemony over the politics of the North Atlantic, with its derivative discourse of neoliberalism. The political cult of neoliberalism, especially its austerity derivative, has impacted the potency of biopower and the State which has resulted in the growing challenges to political mainstream orthodoxy by alternate political discourses rooted in neo-fascism and neo-Nazism, with political orthodoxy seeking to steal the thunder from the alternate challengers. All aspects of the political orthodoxy are now under assault, including the changes to the four lines of assault on sex.

Discursive hegemony is predicated on seeking out, incentivising and replicating difference and diversity for it is the only means by which resistance can be ferreted out, exposed and neutralised. Politics that thrives on the discourse of the Luddites pose a grave threat to biopower, and the politics of the assault on the political mainstream in the North Atlantic is the extreme form of the discourse of the Luddites; whilst austere neoliberalism, with its cult of the free market, has already impacted the potency of biopower by dismantling the State and reducing the operational space of biopower, given the grave clash between the discourse and technologies of power of biopower and the discourse and technology of power of neoliberalism in all its variants. In this terrain, the politics of neoliberalism now trumps the politics of biopower to the detriment of social control reflected in the embrace of militarised, racist policing which singularly targets the diversity and difference that must be generated by biopower. In the 21ˢᵗ century biopower is now under assault in the political realm from its most potent challenger to appear to date since the late nineteenth century. What is painfully clear is that neoliberalism in its hegemonic position cannot ensure the integrity of the social order, as it simply does not have the ability nor the technology of power to do so. As it has no technology of the body of its own for it is a discourse of limited applicability, vision and worldview, manifested by the willingness and propensity to erode the basis of social control for the material benefit of a visible, ostentatious local and global oligarchy. What it has then embraced as its solution is racist war, both internally and externally, for hegemonic neoliberalism has embraced the right to make live and allow to live in a manner that is akin to national socialism and the slave plantation, rather than that of Enlightenment liberalism. The resurgence of neo-Fascism and neo-Nazism in the electoral politics of the North Atlantic in the 21ˢᵗ century is then the product of the crisis of hegemonic neoliberalism in its assault on biopower. This assault is being played out in the politics of the North Atlantic and what is now apparent in the second decade of the 21ˢᵗ century is hegemonic austere neoliberalism has now embraced a strain of white supremacist discourse to drive its biopower noted for its paranoid, siege mentality, extremist, militarist stance in defence of Empire which indicates a biopower now in operational crisis. The hegemony of neoliberalism, intensified by the political cult of neoliberalism, has exposed the sophistry at the core of bourgeois hegemonic discourse. Bourgeois discourse has a fundamental distrust of freedom, but was forced to accept the compromise afforded by biopower, where the object of power is free to choose from a menu of choices constituted by biopower. But hegemonic financial market neoliberalism, driven by the political cult of neoliberalism, is assaulting the operational effectiveness of biopower by illustrating graphically the discourse of truth/the lies of power that drive the policing of the social order, which impacts the ability of biopower to seduce the individual to police themselves. With its penchant for predatory behaviour that threatens the stability of the social order and the grave instances of social inequality that is the product of wilful strategy, hegemonic neoliberal discourse has now placed on the agenda the freedom to choose resistance; and in response it has launched a war on freedom by deploying a biopower driven by a paranoid strain of white supremacist discourse with a siege mentality to suppress freedom to choose resistance. But neoliberalism cannot help itself, and the political cult ensures that the fissures in the order will deepen further, exposing the sophistry of hegemonic discourse. For the politics of the North Atlantic cannot relegate neoliberalism to its strategic space in hegemonic bourgeois discourse, in the chorus of subjugated knowledges, for it was politicians who enabled its resurgence and hegemony, to the detriment of the hegemony of the North Atlantic and the continuity of its social order from the nineteenth century to the present. The discourse of race war, retooled and reformulated as an instrument of hegemonic neoliberal discourse, is then back and in vogue with the promise of apocalypse now!

Chapter Nine
The Discourse of West Indian Slavery

This chapter is presented to confirm the dire need to be informed of the discourse of African enslavement in the West Indies and its impact on the evolution of the discourse of race war in Europe. In this chapter a deconstruction of the discourse is presented with reference to its technology of power and power relations that forms part of a wider study that is in train, a work in progress. The power relations of the slave States of the West Indies in fact expose the various terrains the discourse was forced to adapt to and operate in. There were the power relations of the unique West Indian production unit, the plantation, where massa was in involved in power relations with the enslaved, the white employees of the plantation and the free African and Mulatto employees of the plantation. Massa was enmeshed in power relations with the colonial State, the local political power structure, other whites as fellow planters, merchants, white labour and free African and Mulatto labour and most importantly with the commission agent who funded the annual costs of the plantation in lieu of the receipt of raw sugar as payment. Massa was then enmeshed in an intricate and complex web of power relations which demanded a strategic road map. What must be accepted is that the plantation was a unit of capitalist production rooted in enslaved labour the population of which dominated the population of the slave colony. A plantation produced raw sugar which was exported to the colonial metropole and sold to cover the debt to the commission agent with the difference repatriated to the massa. The market price for raw sugar impacted the profitability and viability of the plantation. The indebtedness of the massa to the commission agent was the next grave threat to profitability. A massa unable to match expenditure to revenue soon fell by the wayside. But the cost structure of production was largely outside of the control of massa as labour was imported from West Africa and sold by globalised traders to massa and all other production inputs were imported as labour was. As a capitalist unit of production the production costs must be reduced to raise revenue but the cost of labour was set by globalised traders not the labour market of the colony. This will only begin to change with the outlawing of the slave trade in the British Empire/colonies in 1807 and the period of restriction and curtailment in the French Empire/colonies from the 1815 Congress of Vienna to the 1831 French legislation.

Massa was then called upon to be a multi skilled actor in the quest for sustainable wealth generation as a producer of raw sugar. The primary issue was the use of effective means of control where the absolute power of the white massa is assured towards generating wealth by exploiting the enslaved African labour of the plantation. The massa was also personally dependent on enslaved African labour for his personal comforts and that of his family and in the daily bump and grind of power relations on the plantation massa became very dependent on key personalities of the various aggregations of the enslaved work force. Members of the primary field work gang, members of the factory work force, members of the ancillary work gangs, members of the care givers and healers and especially members of the domestic enslaved. Throughout these power relations the issue of which choice in the range of possible actions: force, brutality and power/ persuasion/motivation was always present especially so in light of the ever present grave fear of the enslaved African majority vis-à-vis the security of the white minority. One indicator of this was the paranoia over poison. Massa then responded differently in keeping with various factors but the prime directive was always ensuring the maintenance of white power in the face of African threats and belligerence defined and limited by the need for the survival of the production unit as a viable wealth generation unit. This was an operational minefield open to extremism on all sides which eventually ended capitalist production of raw sugar rooted in enslaved labour in the West Indian colonies. The capitalist unit of production demanded a base of production that was free of the extreme power relations of the slave plantation and the enslaved African singlehandedly engineered this collapse with their resistance to enslavement. The most potent blow to this enterprise was the Haitian Revolution of 1804.

This chapter will deconstruct the discourse of the journal of Maria Nugent, wife of the Governor of Jamaica from 1801-1805 as it affords the discourse of a person at the core of colonial power in Jamaica in the period. This is the discourse of a woman who was not a West Indian native in fact Maria Nugent was a native of the then British colony of New Jersey subsequently a state of the USA raised in an Episcopalian Christian household. The other work is the letters and diary of Pierre Dessalles 1808-1856 a planter/massa of Martinique, French colonial West Indies where only a specific amount of letters will be deconstructed.

Lady Nugent's Journal

1801

"The ladies told me strange stories of the influence of the black and yellow women and Mrs. Bullock called them serpents" (Wright 2002 pg.12).

"They are all so good humoured, and seem so merry, that it is quite comfortable to look at them. I wish, however, they would be a little more alert in clearing away the filth of this otherwise nice and fine house." (Wright 2002 pg. 13).

"Reflect all night upon slavery, and make up my mind, that the want of exertion in the blackies must proceed from that cause. Assemble them after breakfast, and talk to them a great deal, promising every kindness and indulgence. We parted excellent friends, and I think they have been rather more active in cleaning ever since." (Wright 2003 pg. 14)

"Had a learned conversation on the cultivation of sugar-canes, the population of negroes, &c. Mr. C. told me he gave two dollars to every woman who produced a healthy child; but no marriages were thought of!!" (Wright 2002 pg. 26).

"After the usual breakfast, gave my last lecture to the blackies, and finished my Christian story. I consider them now so well acquainted with their expected duties, that I have appointed the Rev. Mr. Warren to be here to-morrow at 12, for the purpose of baptising them." (Wright 2002 pg. 38).

For the year 1801, the year of arrival in Jamaica Mary Nugent finds the house enslaved at the residence of the Governor indolent, lazy and shirking their duties as a result of being enslaved. But in spite of this they are merry and good humoured. Mary Nugent's strategy to manage the power relations created between the enslaved and herself is to convert all of them to Christianity towards using Christian discourse as the definer of the terrain of engagement. The enslaved then pledge allegiance as enslaved Christians to a white Christian woman their superior and the white Christian woman will in return treat them with kindness and indulgences. The baptism of the enslaved as Christians in no way ends their enslavement nor does it change the race grounded power relations. In fact, it cannot insulate and protect the enslaved Christians from the power relations of the slave society as their sale to another slave owner and the shattering of their families through the sale of the adults, their partner and/ or children. This then is a strategy of power devised by Mary Nugent for her own benefit and in its application she betrays a common feature of the journals of slave owners: self-delusional denial. Where she is convinced she has hustled the enslaved Africans failing to grasp that the jigaboo routine was designed by the African to hustle white people. Mary Nugent is then a racist as she has no problem with the actual order of enslavement of Africans as they are a race worthy of enslavement by whites. What she is concerned with is the lack of a Christian veneer placed over the entire order such as paying those who reproduce but they are reproducing out of wedlock. Her concern with the Christian veneer does not form the basis of any rejection of the enslavement of African Christians for enslaved African Christians are not the real deal for Africans are not the same with whites and Christianity is for the whites. Enslaved African Christians are then the children of a lesser god.

1802

"Set all the blackies to scrape and clean all-round the house, the lawn, &c. Treated them with beef and punch, and never was there a happier set of people that they appear to be. All day they have been singing odd songs, only interrupted by peals of laughter; and indeed I must say they have reason to be content, for they have many comforts and enjoyments. I only wish the poor Irish were half as well off." (Wright 2002 pg. 53).

"One little black girl came to beg that I would take her with me. She was a remarkably thick-lipped and ugly, but intelligent child. She could say the Lord's Prayer perfectly, but could not tell how she had learnt it; both her father and mother are field negroes, and neither of them can say their prayers." (Wright 2002 pg. 69).

"Nelly Nugent remarked, however, that it was astonishing how fast these black women bred, what healthy children they had, and how soon they recovered after lying-in. Indeed, I have heard medical men make the same observation." (Wright 2002 pg.69).

"Amused myself with reading the evidence before the House of Commons, on the part of the petitioners for the Abolition of the Slave Trade. As far as I at present see and hear of the ill treatment of the slaves, I think what they say upon the subject is very greatly exaggerated. I believe the slaves are extremely well used." (Wright 2002 pg. 86).

"Yet it appears to me, there would be certainly no necessity for the Slave Trade, if religion, decency, and good order, were established among the negroes; if they could be prevailed upon to marry; and if our white men would set them a little better example." (Wright 2002 pg. 86).

"Mrs Bell told me to-day, that a negro man and woman of theirs, who are married, have fourteen grown up children, all healthy field negroes. This is only one instance out of many, which proves, that, the climate of this country being more congenial to their constitutions, they would increase and render the necessity of the Slave Trade out of the question," (Wright 2002 pgs. 86-87).

"provided their masters were attentive to their morals and established matrimony among them; but white men of all descriptions, married or single, live in a state of licentiousness with their female slaves; and until a reformation takes place on their part, neither religion, decency, nor morality, can be established among the negroes. (Wright 2002 pg. 87).

"Have an old negro man here, who was coachman to Lord Portland, when he was Governor of this island in 1721. He is still healthy and active, and this reminds me of an old woman, who died while we were in St Mary's, who was so old that no one could tell her exact age; but, from known circumstances, she had certainly seen her 140th year! Does not this prove how congenial the climate is to their colour?" (Wright 2002 pg. 96).

"It is extraordinary to witness the immediate effect that the climate and the habit of living in this country have upon the minds and manners of Europeans, particularly of the lower orders. In the upper ranks, they become indolent and inactive, regardless of everything but eating, drinking, and indulging themselves, and are almost entirely under the domination of their mulatto favourites." (Wright 2002 pg. 98).

"In the lower orders, they are the same, with the addition of conceit and tyranny; considering the negroes as creatures formed merely to their ease, and subject to their caprice; and I have found much difficulty to persuade those great people and superior beings, our white domestics, that the blacks are human beings, or have souls. I allude more particularly to our German and our other upper men-servants." (Wright 2002 pg. 98).

"The blackies perfect in their prayers. Read to them myself this evening, and intent doing so in the future." (Wright 2002 pg. 103).

In 1802 Mary Nugent sets about the task of formulating a discourse of biopolitics for the preservation of capitalist production rooted in African enslavement. Nugent took great pains in presenting her case that the African thrives in the climate of the Jamaica seen in the long life of Africans and the fertility of and the rapid post pregnancy and delivery recovery of the African female. Mary Nugent in her application of her Christian values based and driven system of the Governor's residence indicated that it is possible to have happy, merry well taken care of enslaved Africans whose lot in life is superior to that of the free, white Irish. Nugent's biopolitics is necessary to generate a sustainable social order where the enslaved reproduce themselves at the necessary volume to end the need for the African slave trade. This technology of power of Mary Nugent is premised on the application of the Christian order, values and norms, to the present social order where Africans will remain enslaved but they are Christian enslaved Africans. Christian enslaved Africans must be participants of key Christian values and norms as conversion, marriage, reproduction and sexual activity within marriage and the application of Christian values and norms to all relations with the African enslaved. Christian discourse will then constitute docile Africans who willingly police themselves according to Christian values and norms. It is then a technology of power that combines the disciplinary with the regulatory and the right to graphic barbaric violence present and lurking in the background. But Nugent in 1802 recognises the grave difficulty in having this technology of power adopted by the social order namely the hierarchical order of white society. Nugent insists that the climate and power of impunity afforded whites by African enslavement have mutated the whites into depraved individuals as they are no longer European Christians. For Nugent the sexual activity of white males especially males of the white elite with non-white women especially the Mulatto women was the prime indicator of white male depravity in Jamaica. Nugent in 1801 and 1802 did not speak of white male sexual activity with African enslaved women as her fixation was on the attractiveness of women of mixed race to white males. The products of coupling across the racial divide were the prized sexual targets of white males which impacted the power relations between white women and white males and between white women and African and Mulatto women. Sexuality and power relations were then impacted by the discourse of race and sexual prowess. African women who were physically suited to the climate seen in their physical prowess and fertility were also adept sexual beings. The Mulatto woman then posed the gravest threat to the white female as she carried the characteristics of the white race and those of the African which when mixed in the right proportion a white woman simply could not compete with. A social order in which racist myths generated operational reality.

Nugent the apologist for African enslavement responds to the threat posed by the campaign of the abolitionists but Nugent finds the little African girl ugly and noted her lips but the child is intelligent because she learnt the Lord's Prayer unlike her parents. But Nugent does not record any problem with the child being separated from her parents. Such is the nature of the racist agenda of Nugent as she personally benefits from the order of enslavement as England does as the colony exists to be exploited by the oligarchs of England. This power relation created the post her husband George Nugent was appointed to.

1803

"After dinner explore the negro houses. Most of them neat, and very comfortable, with poultry," (Wright 2002 pg. 154).

"I began the ball with an old negro man. The gentlemen each selected a partner, according to rank, by age or service, and we all danced. However, I was not aware how much I shocked the Misses Murphy by doing this; for I did exactly the same as I would have done at a servants' hall birthday in England." (Wright 2002 pg. 156).

"They told me, afterwards, that they were nearly fainting, and could hardly forbear shedding a flood of tears, at such an unusual and extraordinary sight; for in this country, and among slaves, it was necessary to keep up so much distant respect!" (Wright 2002 pg. 156).

"They may be right. I meant nothing wrong, and all the poor creatures seemed so delighted, and so much pleased, that I could scarcely repent it. I was, nevertheless very sorry to have hurt their feelings, and particularly too as they seemed to think the example dangerous; as making the blacks of too much consequence, or putting them at all on a footing with the whites, they said might make a serious change in their conduct, and even produce a rebellion in the island." (Wright 2002 pg. 156).

"In the evening, many unpleasant and alarming reports, respecting the French prisoners on parole and the negroes in this town. This, together with the rumours all day, of an understanding between the French prisoners and the free blacks, and their tampering with the negro slaves, was indeed most frightful. (Wright 2002 pg. 187).

"I cannot describe the anxiety I suffered, nor the thousand horrid ideas that pressed upon my mind; and, especially, as there had appeared of late a general apprehension throughout the country, and various reports have been made, within the last few weeks; of the alarming state of the negro population." (Wright 2002 pg. 187).

Mary Nugent in 1803 deepens her application of her strategy to discipline the enslaved at the Governor's residence by organising a ball for the enslaved where she commenced the dancing with an enslaved aged African male. The white females present of the Murphy family expressed their grave horror at Nugent's deliberate flouting of the race demarcated boundaries established between especially white women and African males. Nugent's take on the opposition posed by the Murphy white women was the position expressed that to challenge the race demarcation of space and contact poses a grave threat to the stability of the colony. Nugent rejected this position outright. What is apparent here is the power relations that were impacting the actions of Nugent. As the wife of the Governor she was expected to do all in her power to preserve the slave social order as defined by the white minority. The views expressed to Nugent on the occasion of the ball for the enslaved of the Governor's residence was then an assault on her disciplinary and biopower agendas. In this instance two discourses of slavery and the policing of the enslaved were in conflict. Mary Nugent the wife of the Governor was then utilising the power of the apex post of the colonial political structure to dismiss such criticism and continue with her agenda. A privilege another white woman with a vastly different class position would have paid the price for so doing. The Murphy discourse in 1803 is hegemonic and it exhibits a morbid, paranoid fear of ever present, imminent genocide perpetuated by the enslaved African majority on the powered white minority. The African has then to be put and kept in his and her space as defined and allocated to them by the massa and these spaces must be ruthlessly policed for failure to do so will signal the weakness of the whites and trigger their genocide. The African has then to be the recipient of public, graphic, barbaric violence as this is the only means to preserve white entitlement. But simultaneously the Africans are a vital and necessary investment in a capitalist enterprise that demands sustainability to generate wealth through the maximisation of profits. The grave failure of this vital investment to reproduce itself forcing an annual investment in the purchase of newly imported enslaved Africans or the purchase of Africans on a secondary market presented the most potent threat to the capitalist enterprise. This capitalist enterprise therefore demanded the application of the two technologies of power. Why then were they never applied? The slave plantation was then by its structure schizoid.

In 1803 it was the turn of Mary Nugent to experience the paranoia generated by the expectation of white genocide in a slave colony. The realities of the Haitian Revolution, both local and geopolitical, were now washing over Jamaica and in this scenario there was a hierarchy of grave threats perceived by the white minority. Threat number 1 was that posed by the free Africans, threat number 2 by the French and both threats combined will release the holocaust by stirring up a slave rebellion of the Haitian model. Mary Nugent was the wife of the Governor and the Governor George Nugent was a military governor placing her at the centre of power and the knowledge of the existing capacity to resist and overcome such a rebellion. From 1803 to her departure in 1805 Mary Nugent was constantly mindful of the threats posed and reacted to them. But Nugent was not a native of the colony and there was always the expectation of a posting out of Jamaica. This morbid fear, even paranoia over imminent white genocide raises the question of the sustainability of joining capitalist enterprise with enslaved labour. Clearly the "rational" demands of capitalism repeatedly fell on deaf ears as the morbid fear and paranoia over imminent white genocide and the barbarity utilised thereof silenced the "rational" demands of capitalism.

1804-September 3, 1805

"Hear all the new blackies their prayers, &c, previously to their being made Christians." (Wright 2002 pg. 215).

"At 7 o'clock, all repaired to the chapel, where all the new servants, and infants lately born, were baptised, and I trust in God, they may turn out good Christians, and peaceable members of society at least; for I have tried to make them understand their duty." (Wright 2002 pg. 215).

"but she tells me that, before she left Spanish Town, the negroes appeared to be inclined to riot, and to make a noise in the streets, when the troops marched out, they were soon dispersed by the militia. The black servants here seem to rejoice at the bustle, but, as they profess to hate the French, their pleasure is only that of change; for, like children, they are fond of fuss and noise, and have no reflection." (Wright 2002 pg. 226).

"We met a horrid looking black man, who passed us several times, without making any bow," "He was then very humble, but to-night he only grinned, and gave us a sort of fierce look, that struck me with a terror I could not shake off." "Clifford tells me that all of the black people know there is some alarm, but are ignorant of the cause of it, and most of them, it is to be feared, are ready for every sort of mischief. However, I feel confident in our own servants, who all seem as anxious to secure the house, and to be as much afraid of depredations, as I am." (Wright 2002 pg. 227).

"My spirits are not a little depressed, as he hinted the necessity of perhaps sending me and the dear children into the interior of the island," "but I am sure that the blacks are to be as much dreaded as the French." (Wright 2002 pg. 237).

"as the interior of the island is now considered the safest place. So it certainly is, from the French, but how will they guard against the insurrection of the negroes." (Wright 2002 pg. 237).

"I have been told, by the few ladies who remain in Spanish Town, such horrid things of the savage ideas, &c, of the slaves, on the estates in the interior, that I am determined, if my dear N. is obliged to leave me to meet the enemy, that I will take my dear children on board a ship, or anywhere near the coast, from where we may make our escape, rather than accept of the asylum offered me by Mr. Mitchell, &c. &c." (Wright 2002 pg. 240).

"On his estate, he has christened all his negroes, and has induced many of them to marry, and lead regular lives. He says, they have in consequence improved in all respects; are sober, quiet and well behaved; and the last year twelve children were born of parents regularly married. The new negroes are attended to, the instant they arrive on the estate, and are taught their prayers most zealously, by the older black Christians, and those best instructed and most capable. How delightful this is! I wish to God it could be made general, and I am sure the benefits arising from it, in every point of view, would be incalculable." (Wright 2002 pg. 242).

Mary Nugent is continuing with her agenda to operationalise her two technologies of power on the enslaved of the Governor's residence. Whilst the paranoia generated by the threat of imminent white genocide at the hands of the enslaved Africans heightens. Nugent is now very sensitive to enslaved Africans whose attitude of docility and respect have now changed for aggression and has decided that in the event of a French attack on Jamaica she will not seek safety in the interior of Jamaica as this will expose her children and her to the ravages of the African enslaved of the interior. The slave order is then under attack by the African enslaved threatening the sustainability of the colonial enterprise and the safety of Mary Nugent and her family. Again

Nugent betrays her support of the colonial slave order and the fact that her strategy of the two technologies of power is a necessary intervention to ensure the sustainability of the colonial slave enterprise. Why then was the strategy of Nugent or any other strategy of the two technologies of power incapable of being applied to the colonial slave enterprise? Nugent cites the evidence in the 1804-1805 period of Christian enslaved Africans being the necessary and requisite model for the sustainability of the capitalist slave enterprise. And biopower is addressing the mortality and fertility rates of the enslaved Africans where more children will be produced and survive to adulthood swelling the ranks of the enslaved. This twin technology of power is rooted in Christian discourse with its values and norms. Nugent is then identifying plantation owners who are applying the technologies of power independently and of their own volition on their plantations with success. But there is no rule to insist that these technologies of power must be applied across the social order and she is of the opinion this never will materialise.

From the journal entries presented for the years 1803 and 1804-1805 the vast difference between white racism in Jamaica under the slave order and white racism in the American south under the slave order is apparent. A visible white minority in Jamaica lived in constant fear of imminent genocide especially with the onset of the Haitian Revolution. The internecine warfare between European nations from the French Revolution (1789) to the Congress of Vienna (1815) heightened this paranoia with the threat of invasion and occupation triggering mini Haitian Revolutions in the rest of the Caribbean. By dint of its minority demographic position whites in Jamaica during the period of Nugent's journal (1801-1805) exhibited an uneasy white supremacist racism where they were always seeking out signs, portents and indicators of the ever expected African backlash. This fed into a discourse of race hate and racist vengeance which dehumanised the enslaved African by reducing her/him to clichés incapable of resistance yet capable of genocide in a fit of barbaric blood lust. White racist extremist barbarity then set the stage that all resistance must in turn return in kind as illustrated by the Haitian Revolution. This discourse will never embrace the strategic need for the operationalisation of the two technologies of power which condemned the capitalist enterprise tied to enslavement to consummate failure. But the answer lies in the nature of the State and its politics both locally and geopolitically.

The State in Jamaica was a vassal, dependent state of the State of the colonial metropole. This dependent colonial State's primary strategic goal was to attain the agenda set by the colonial metropole which meant that the colonial State of Jamaica was not organic to the power relations of the Jamaican social order in the nineteenth century during the stint of Mary Nugent and thereafter. The colonial vassal State was not the macro institution that drove the hegemonic discourse and the technologies of power of the social order. It simply sat as the conqueror at the apex of the society demanding tribute be exported to the metropole. Faced with the abolition movement in Britain with the assault on slavery in Britain, the slave trade and abolition of slavery all accomplished legislatively by 1833 the vassal colonial State did nothing in response to these threats to push for a new order in Jamaica. In the nineteenth century in Jamaica the white minority persisted with a seventeenth and eighteenth century discourse of white racist supremacist, paranoid, barbaric, African slavery. A hegemonic discourse that failed to understand that the issue was sustainable wealth generation not white racism and domination of inferior races. Which failed to engage with the threats posed to the social order they desired by political developments in the colonial metropole. Further proof of the rationalism of capitalism being a bourgeois invention simply a discourse of truth where in Jamaica paranoid white racist supremacy trumped the capitalist imperative. The fact that the colonial State and the State of the colonial metropole from 1838 to independence in 1962 maintained the hegemony of the discourse of white racist supremacy and the technology of power devoted to constituting docile non-whites, who were alienated from themselves viewing the world and themselves through white constructs illustrates the continuity of the racist worldview as the cement that binds the matrix of the social order. This is a State and a social order that has no need in the 21st century for disciplinary and biopower as the plantation order has proven sustainable across time with its hierarchy of non-African races forming the Jamaican oligarchy to the exclusion of members of the majority African race still in robust existence in the 21st century. Bourgeois hegemonic discourse with its two technologies of power

140

are then not the universal norm, as in the case of colonial and neo-colonial Jamaica this is not the norm as the hegemonic discourse that was displaced by bourgeois hegemonic discourse through political actions in the metropole was never displaced and replaced in Jamaica by bourgeois hegemonic discourse. The hegemonic discourse of the plantation order was simply reformulated and applied in the post-enslavement colonial era under the leadership of the colonial State to the detriment of the power wielded by the adherents of plantation white, racist supremacy. In exchange for maintaining the plantation order and social hierarchy based on docile, cheap non-white labour the white minority was forced to surrender to the dictates of the colonial conqueror State. Out of this power relation came the introduction of immigration schemes to import docile, cheap labour into the colonies from the Empire to ensure the docility and the right price of indigenous African labour. The British Colonial State was then a racist, white, supremacist State in their colonies of the West Indies intent on exploiting these colonies via a lumpen capitalist order dominated by the white race and policing a racist social hierarchy where the white minority dominated the apex/the oligarchy of the structure. Capitalist exploitation in an organic embrace with white racist supremacy and a colonial, imperialist, white, racist, supremacist State. Such is the legacy of British colonial imperialism in the West Indies.

Such is the nature then of the pressing need to map the impact such developments in the Caribbean had on the evolution of discourse and technologies of power in Europe and the State from the seventeenth to the nineteenth centuries. The colonial States formulated, applied and evolved under European colonial imperialism will then potently illustrate the masked nature of power and power relations in European political discourse of the colonial metropoles. The bare, naked fully exposed and manifested reality of the European Colonial States in all its white, racist, supremacist livery is in fact the masked reality of the North Atlantic State.

The Letters of Pierre Dessalles of Martinique

This study will concentrate on letters from 1822 to 1826 written by Pierre Dessalles to his mother in France the substantive owner of the plantation in Martinique and former resident of Martinique.

20 April 1822

"We are making sugar, although the cane does not yield as much as we expected. We still have a large number of negroes in the hospital, but not one of them is seriously ill." (Forster and Forster 1996 pg. 45).

"One notices that Europeans, who cry out so loudly against the barbarity of the colonial planters, are usually much harsher than the Creoles themselves. This is because they do not know the infernal race whom we have to guide" (Forster and Forster 1996 pg. 46).

16 July 1822

"Everything is going beautifully at the plantation, the negroes are behaving well, and I have every reason to believe that our revenue will be assured with 7,000 to 8,000 moulds of sugar." (Forster and Forster 1996 pg. 46

"I am going to marry five couples; Germain and Laurance, Saint-Cyr and Marie-Barnabe, Jean-Pierre and Jeanne-Rose (who has just given birth to two children), Edouard-Bibianne and Adrienne and La-fortune and Monique. I am giving them advantages that will turn to our benefit and re-establish morality. To my mind, this is the only way to ward off evil and bad intentions. The future will tell if I am mistaken." (Forster and Forster 1996 pg. 46).

"Slaves from other places and free mulattoes are not to come to the plantation." (Forster and Forster 1996 pg.46).

11 August 1822

"The Lamentin district is ablaze right now; poison is causing horrendous ravages." (Forster and Forster 1996 pg. 48).

"Madame Champ cannot get over the beauty of the negro children and the healthy look of the adults." (Forster and Forster 1996 pg. 48).

8 September 1822

"The kind of individuals the government sends us makes it clear that it is not interested in the colonies." "Since protection of its colonies is not among

France's concerns, the generous thing would be to let the colonists devise the means to protect themselves against the evils that threaten them." (Forster and Forster 1996 pg. 49).

18 October 1822

"The government wants to do us in, and we have ample proof of it," "What is needed would be to be firm in dealing with a certain class and, in particular, never permit a mulatto to return once he had left it. Communications with Saint- Domingue takes place every day." (Forster and Forster 1996 pgs. 49-50).

"If I am to believe some of the negroes, I can count on all of them. It is worth a great deal that they voice such good intentions, but I have little faith that good can come from such an evil race." (Forster and Forster 1996 pg. 50).

30 December 1822

"I have lost two adult negroes, Lapin and Philoge, and two children. This does not diminish the number of workers, but I am far from saying, as some people do, that this just means fewer mouths to feed. Whatever shape he may be in, a negro is always doing something and must be replaced if he is gone." (Forster and Forster 1996 pg. 51).

Dessalles accepts the reality that the wealth generation capacity of the capitalist entity that produces raw sugar for export to the colonial metropole is entirely dependent on the productivity of the enslaved Africans. The problem for Dessalles to solve on a day by day basis is the strategy to devise and deploy that assures the productivity of persons held against their will, persons forced to generate wealth with no compensation due to them. In addition, Dessalles has to devise a strategy to deal with resistance that spans a spectrum of human action from passive resistance to murder and at the apex genocide both African and white. Placed in the context of the colony Dessalles has to deal with the role of the colonial State in securing the colony and the threats posed internally and externally. Dessalles is living in and walking through a minefield.

Dessalles describes the African as an infernal and evil race primarily because of their resistance to enslavement and in this categorisation the Haitian

Revolution is the grave threat always battering his consciousness. Dessalles in 1822 walks his strategy on the ground by marrying enslaved couples to send a message of reward and stability for those who work to the standard policed by him. In this he also wants to raise the number of children born to the enslaved and survive into adulthood. Dessalles is then expecting enslaved Africans to willingly procreate and willingly raise their children as slaves for the benefit of massa. Dessalles is relying on a web of personal patronage that moves outwards from his persona which seeks to enmesh all persons on the plantation into a matrix of power relations with him. All power then resides in Dessalles solely and those who challenge his imperial power will be dealt with including the white employees. Through this matrix of power relations Dessalles sets about the task of creating a cadre of enslaved Africans throughout all the work gangs of the enslaved who report directly and personally to him and project his power via their bodies into the spaces where they inhabit. In exchange they are rewarded and Dessalles takes pride in the quality of the care he affords his enslaved. But there must be another side to Dessalles the side that handles resistance and rebellion.

What is noteworthy in 1822 is that every enslaved African mentioned in his letters has a French name and is of importance to the strategic intent of Dessalles including the children hence his knowledge of their life situation. Dessalles was then executing a strategy of the cultural and worldview modification of those enslaved Africans he considered of strategic importance to him. This had nothing to do with house slave and field slave and the false dichotomy it generates it was based on the strategic importance the enslaved African held in the social order of the plantation for Dessalles.

Dessalles has a grave problem with the threat posed by the existence of Haiti in 1822 seen in the fact that he still uses the old French colonial designation Saint-Domingue. He is insisting that there are links between the colony and Haiti and the prime threat is posed by the Mulattoes of the colony as they are the agents of the agenda to replicate the Haitian model in Martinique. Dessalles wants the Mulattoes surveilled by the State and those who travel abroad banned from returning to the colony as they are carrying the virus. But the colonial State is failing in its duty as its personnel are inadequate to the task at hand and Dessalles envisions a process of localisation of the personnel of the colonial State as the solution needed hence a power grab. The product of coupling across the racial divide, the Miscegenated of slavery is now for Dessalles posing a grave threat to the survival of the slave colony.

1823

6 January 1823

"Today the government must make its position perfectly clear and no longer give hopes to a class that will never pass up an opportunity to revolt. The conspiracy was serious; all the whites were to be massacred," (Forster and Forster 1996 pg. 52-53).

"It has been decided that no more manumissions are to be authorised." (Forster and Forster 1996 pg. 53).

26 March 1823

"Sacriste hanged himself and I lost Baron, Elie, and poor little Delie, whom I miss very much. She was attached to her masters and would have grown up to be a good subject." (Forster and Forster 1996 pg. 53).

4 July 1823

"I always have between 30 and 40 negroes in the hospital. Twelve have died since January, and several others are threatening to die. This is not normal, but I keep up my courage," (Forster and Forster 1996 pg. 55).

"Praxcede says that she is pregnant, but her pregnancy does not show yet. As long as she is promiscuous anyway, I would at least like her to have many children who would someday make good slaves for us. Praxcede always behaves well, she is running everything in the house and especially in my room: she is eager and faithful. Edouard is the best negro one has ever seen, and Celicour will follow in his footsteps. Foiry is a good negro," (Forster and Forster 1996 pg. 53).

"The kinds of people who inhabit the colonies are not like those in France; and so the prefect, before implementing his intentions and before taking steps to restore morality, which had been entirely forgotten by the people of colour, should have thought about the interests of the colonial system." "and let himself be convinced that the established order must be preserved if slavery and the respect that free people of colour owe the whites are to be maintained." (Forster and Forster 1996 pg. 56).

"The people of colour and the negroes have no belief in the truth of religion; they are thinking about one thing only; and that is the destruction of the whites and the overthrow of the government." (Forster and Forster 1996 pg. 56).

"I no longer allow any slave from the outside on the place, nor any free blacks. All these communications are dangerous." (Forster and Forster 1996 pg. 57).

26 July 1823

"Our negroes continue to torment me." "On the eve of my name day, I indicated that I would not accept the good wishes of any negro." "I have just spent a whole week at the Cafeiere. Several delegations came to see me, led by our most notable subjects." "Cesaire told me, 'give us the devil, if you can, but do not keep M. Chignac. You do not have poison on your place, and discouragement is the only cause of all your troubles." "'Cesaire has killed himself by throwing himself down from the top of the mill wheel.'" (Forster and Forster 1996 pgs. 57-58).

"Actually, everything was in good order, and the work gang did not show any kind of sorrow about this event." "Since January, this Cesaire has been accused by several negroes of having giving them poison." (Forster and Forster 1996 pg.58).

"I shall play my role to the very end. To dismiss Chignac would be to show weakness, yet he cannot stay with me much longer. He himself will eventually ask to be let go, this is what I am working on. Unfortunately, this Chignac is a brute," (Forster and Forster 1996 pg. 59).

"I was able to buy 27 negroes both adults and children, all of them Creoles, on very easy terms." "It will provide home grown food for all the negroes, a labour force to maintain the revenue of the sugar mill, as well as a certain quantity of coffee which when sold in France, will always fetch better prices than the shipments of sugar." (Forster and Forster 1996 pg. 59).

"Some good individuals can be found among our slaves, but many are bad. I am pleased with the house slaves; they are all well. Edouard is worth his weight in gold," (Forster and Forster 1996 pg. 60).

13 September 1823

"but one must never shout victory, for the race of men we must command is diabolical and treacherous." "Romauld he confessed to having committed grave crimes," "I asked him about the work gang, and he named Cesaire, Raymond and Eulalie as the only ones who had caused us to suffer losses." "This Raymond met an end very similar to that of Cesaire, for he threw himself from the top of one of the breadfruit trees in the provisioning ground and died on the spot. Romauld told me positively that Eulalie had sworn that no black baby would ever come to anything as long as she was on the plantation. Two days after she said that, I lost Vitaline's little girl and Helene's, the prettiest little negro children we had on the place, and they died of very strange illnesses. Romauld died after he had received confession." "Now I must deal with Eulalie;" "This criminal woman is astonishingly calm. Five months pregnant she made her belly disappear." (Forster and Forster 1996 pg. 59).

"The hatred against Chignac seems to have died down since I decided to make him head overseer," "I realised that to dismiss him outright would be to yield to the will of people who might well become even more demanding and might even go in for revolt if they noticed the slightest weakness on my part." (Forster and Forster 1996 pgs. 60-61).

"Proprietors must no longer leave their interests," (Forster and Forster 1996 pg. 61).

"An accursed epidemic called Spanish War or vapour, has mown down a prodigious number of negroes, and many whites have also fallen victim to it." (Forster and Forster 1996 pg.62).

10 December 1823

"I just lost Jeanne-Rose, a mother of four children, who was married last year. I had all the last rites administered to her in order to distinguish her from all the others." (Forster and Forster 1996 pg. 62).

"I am not pleased you gave Honore his body; you will be sorry. I will wait before I make such a gift to Dieudonne." (Forster and Forster 1996 pg. 62).

Dessalles in 1823 is now faced with revelations of challenges to his power over the plantation posed by members of the enslaved African population. In spite of his declaration in 1822 and continuing into 1823 that all contact between the enslaved of the plantation and the enslaved and free non-whites external of the plantation are forbidden. Dessalles attempts to isolate the enslaved of the plantation encapsulated in a bubble of his creation and policed by him first Cesaire challenged his power in spite of Cesaire's special status in the work gang by committing a graphic public suicide. Then Romauld served up the second grave cut by confessing to crimes and naming Cesaire, Raymond and Eulalie as fellow enemies of Dessalles all of them his enslaved and special to him especially Eulalie as she apparently was charged with the delivery and care of the new born of the enslaved. Raymond committed public graphic suicide at the provision grounds of the sugar estate in public view rather than surrender and suffer the public fate of Romauld. The gravest blow to Dessalles was what Romauld the informer said of the actions of Eulalie for Dessalles' exercise with biopower was to increase the live births of the enslaved Africans through his strategy which rewarded those who married and had children with special status but child bearing outside of marriage was also expected as the wombs of all enslaved women of child bearing age belonged to Dessalles. Their duty to Dessalles was not complete until they produced children no matter how hard they worked in the other areas expected of them. Dessalles was then formulating a sexuality to encapsulate the bodies of the enslaved Africans thereby facilitating his technology of power charged with policing these bodies. Eulalie then mounted an attack on Dessalles' biopower which sent the message that the wombs of the enslaved must be liberated from Dessalles for enslavement must not pass from generation to generation. One can well imagine the public example Dessalles made of Eulalie to the inmates of Dessalles' bubble as he does not speak of it in his letter to his mother.

In his letters to his mother in 1823 Dessalles reveals his strategy to manage the daily power/force relations of the plantation in his favour. He establishes a discourse of Dessalles as the omnipotent, benevolent dictator where he sits above all the noise of every day power relations as the central, all powerful force of last resort. To lose his favour is then to lose life, for he alone in the space of Dessalles' bubble has the power to kill and to let live and he makes repeated attempts to evolve his power to that of to make live but he simply does not have the required State form to attain that. Dessalles then formulates, unleashes and polices *his discourse of the norm of the negro* which drives his technology of power. Dessalles identifies and grades all the enslaved according to their conditioning by the norm of the negro as there are *"the best negro"*, *"the good negro"* and just "negroes" for all negroes are expected to be treacherous, liars, shirkers, thieves, murderers, godless etc. The negro is the binary opposite of white, and both form the duality of race superiority/white and race inferiority//negro/black. In 1823 Dessalles has reported the most potent assault on his power, his discourse and the technology of power. The suicides of Sacriste, Cesaire and Raymond where the power to kill and let live of Dessalles was seized by three members of the enslaved and the infanticide and murders of Eulalie usurped his prerogative to kill and let live only held by whites over blacks. Whilst Romauld the informer who was granted confession before his execution for crimes against the white omnipotent, benevolent, dictator illustrated the power exerted by the *norm of the negro* of Dessalles' discourse and technology of power in constituting the "*negro*" no longer African now just negro as defined by, and constituted in the image and likeness of white racist hegemonic discourse.

The strategic power game Dessalles plays is also ably illustrated in the case of Chignac the senior white male of France who manages the plantation on a daily basis answerable only to Dessalles. Chignac applies the whip liberally on the plantation Dessalles insists that Chignac is too brutal but he allows Chignac to become the central personification of the evil beke/white man on the plantation. Dessalles has then a white fall guy which enhances his power as all the enslaved through their dominant figures as Cesaire are allowed to approach the benevolent dictator of the plantation seeking redress from the brutality of Chignac. Dessalles then humbles Chignac by demoting him to head overseer whilst he fills the void created, as terminating the employment of Chignac will weaken Dessalles' power over the enslaved as the act reeks of weakness as he would have broken the white line of solidarity. Dessalles finds himself enmeshed in the web of his own making as he has failed to seduce all sides of the power game except himself as he is clearly drunk on the impunity afforded by the power relations of a slave plantation in the West Indies.

In 1823 Dessalles continued his articulation of the threat posed by the State to the sustainability of the colony but he now adds a specific cleric to this list. Colonial officials and a specific cleric, the prefect, in their approach to dealing with the threat posed by the free Mulattoes and blacks are now threatening the very safety of whites in the slave order of the colony. The free non-whites for Dessalles must be policed to ensure that they recognise and show deference to the inherent superiority and dominance of the whites over the colony. And the prefect must understand that all the free Mulattoes and blacks are only interested in white genocide and their rise to power not religion. Dessalles is insisting that these groups are not to be welcomed into the Christian churches as free Christian Mulattoes and blacks are a grave threat to white power. Dessalles in his letters makes no mention of an attempt to Christianise the enslaved in his bubble. In the marriages of the enslaved he frequently includes in his letters he married the enslaved couples.

Dessalles is insisting that the spaces of the slave colony must be demarcated and segregated on the basis of the duality of race, white and black not on the basis of the duality of free and enslaved. Free non-white, non-enslaved persons must be excluded from white spaces as they are not white as only white persons hold the right to and entitlement of freedom the rest were made free by white people and as such this freedom can be taken away by white people. White free space is then sacrosanct and must remain so through the exclusion of non-whites from this space. Dessalles insists that there will be no manumission for the enslaved from his bubble in light of this position and the suspension of manumissions by the administration of the colony. But his mother sends back Honore to the plantation in Martinique from France where he is deployed by Dessalles then she grants Honore his manumission. Dessalles gets a lesson in power as his mother is the substantive owner of the plantation which places him in the position of having others on the plantation now expecting manumission of which ne names one.

Dessalles in 1823 provides details of his pet project of the Cafeiere where he has invested in creating a food crop venture to feed the entire work force of the plantation and to plant, tend and eventually reap ripened coffee beans for export. Dessalles is moving to reduce his overhead costs of purchasing imported food which is a huge cost given some 200 mouths to feed daily eclipsed only by the annual cost of purchasing enslaved labour given the mortality rate of adults and the failure of enslaved labour to reproduce itself. In addition, Dessalles is putting in place another export cash commodity. To this end in 1823 he purchases enslaved adult and children to work at the Cafeiere and the raw sugar factory through long term debt. A debt he is obligated to pay even though the enslaved Africans die before it's amortised. Such are the risks of a capitalist enterprise rooted in enslavement of labour in a social order where the State form is antagonistic even averse to capitalist enterprise. This is no bourgeois State marching in lockstep with capitalism. It is a lesson to the bourgeois of especially Britain and France that their hegemony and the hegemony of capitalism in Europe is only assured with a State form that is appreciative of the specific needs of capitalism. Another potent lesson afforded the discursive agents of the European bourgeoisie is the organic need for capitalism to be rooted in free labour charged with the task of the reproduction of labour which enables the application of biopower by the State. From the fifteenth to the twentieth century the colonial order has always insisted that the plantation order of export capitalism must be rooted in coerced, servile labour where various models were applied from enslavement to contracted immigrant labour.

The lesson is then clear that there must be a State in operational existence legislating and policing these measures that Dessalles conceptualises as being vitally necessary to the sustainability of their capitalist enterprise rooted in enslavement. The colonial slave State was not the necessary state form and in the absence of State policed order there was a series of plantations each with their own specific social order held together by dint of the need for security and by the demands of the capitalist enterprise on a colonial State form predicated on the right of conquest. This was a social order with a State entirely distinct from that of the colonial metropole where it formulated multiple racist discourses with their technologies of power premised on white supremacy exported to the colonial metropole where they were reformulated and operationalised from the seventeenth to the nineteenth centuries. Racist discourses formulated in the colonial West Indies were then at the leading edge of the discursive evolution of the European social order and its State form.

1824

12 March 1824

"I have the satisfaction of telling you that I am infinitely more pleased with the negroes, but they vary so much that I do not dare shout victory." "Your house slaves are behaving well; the little negro will soon be a big negro and follow in the footsteps of his father, with whom I am ever more satisfied." "Celicour is a good fellow," (Forster and Forster 1996 pg. 64).

"As for the apostolic prefect, he will be leaving for France in two months, and all the colonists wish that he will stay there. His religious ideas simply do not fit in with the colonial system." "and it is painful to see that the metropolis does not take a more favourable stance. Everything it does seems to promote the ruin of the colonies." (Forster and Forster 1996 pg. 64).

"Everyone who sees our coffee plantation is astonished. The manager I had there suddenly quit, saying that he no longer wanted to be under Chignac's orders. It is a miserable thing to have a Creole as manager, and it is a risk I will never take again." (Forster and Forster 1996 pg. 64).

26 May 1824

"That is the best I can do, given the obligations I have here. Keep in mind that I have to run and maintain a large property where there is no natural increase whatsoever and for which I have to purchase a certain quantity of negroes every year." "I am expecting my wife; her return to me is absolutely necessary, for it will prove to the world our will to cut all our expenses and our determination to honour all our obligations." "As soon as MM. Durant are paid off, I shall send my wife back to France. If I cannot go with her, I am prepared to sacrifice my person for the good of all my family." (Forster and Forster 1996 pg.66).

"Two of our new negroes have hanged themselves while I was at the session of the court. They were the oldest, those whom M. Gruet had bought from the Spoutourne plantation." (Forster and Forster 1996 pg. 66).

4 July 1824

"all the planters of our district are experiencing the dreadful ravages of poison." "Everything is going perfectly well here, nothing has suffered, the negroes are content and show me their affection." "My principal slaves reassure me. Our prosperity(!!) seems to astonish people, and there are signs of jealousy." (Forster and Forster 1996 pg. 67).

5 July 1824

"Slaves are horrendously expensive, but one must budget the annual purchase of ten negroes in the expenses of the sugar mill. Without that, we cannot possibly continue our business. There are no births, and, although there may be some in the future, we have not had any in a long time, and yet we must produce income." (Forster and Forster 1996 pg. 68).

12-13 July 1824

"Last night at prayer I announced that I would be forced to imitate the severity of my neighbours. All the negroes gave me to understand that the trouble came from the outside; in order to take away all excuses, I cancelled the distribution of tafia." "I have established severe punishments for all outside negroes found on the plantation and for those of ours who receive outsiders in their cabins." (Forster and Forster 1996 pg. 68).

16 July 1824

"and when we opened the cadaver, all the undeniable proofs of poisoning were found." That night, I had 40 lashes administered to the head mule driver. I warned the ploughmen, carters, prairie guards, and the head mule driver that each of them would receive the same punishment every time an animal died." "and that things would not return to normal until they had paid me for the poisoned animals with their work." "They are all submissive, upset, and full of zeal, and I would find it impossible to point to one guilty individual, but it is necessary to show firmness." (Forster and Forster 1996 pgs. 68-69).

"All of this must remain strictly secret. Only our family must know of these events. You do understand that the merchants in France would stop advancing us money, thinking that all is lost." (Forster and Forster 1996 pg.69)

22 July 1824

"The first arrests have been made. The head mule driver of that plantation has accused Eusebe, the guardian of our prairie; I had him arrested." "Eusebe has not yet talked, but I think he will be easy to move. It is proven that there was a plot involving all the head carters and head mule drivers. Eusebe must have accomplices here." "Once the oxen were destroyed, they would have started in on the negroes." "Thanks to my firmness and the severe measures, I have taken, I have stopped our losses." (Forster and Forster 1996 pg. 69).

"Do you realise that it is no small matter having to provide three meals a day to more than 200 individuals?" (Forster and Forster 1996 pg. 69).

24 July 1824

"Eusebe does not want to say anything. I will be sorry to lose this negro; he always worked very hard." (Forster and Forster 1996 pg. 69).

12 August 1824

"The free mulattoes certainly play a role in all this." (Forster and Forster 1996 pg. 71).

15 September 1824

"30 negroes ran away. They were brought back by M. de Seguin, and Jean received 100 lashes." "Jean-Pierre added" "he told me that every year we had eight, ten, twelve, and fourteen pregnancies, but that the negresses got rid of their fruits and that it was known throughout the work gang that Marie-Jeanne had very recently destroyed her child." "All the known poisoners have been warned that, if I lose one man or one animal to poison, I will clap chains on two of them for the rest of their lives, but make sure that they will work hard just the same." (Forster and Forster 1996 pg. 72).

29 September 1824

"I have chains only on Jean-Pierre, Leon, Barthelemy, and Jose." (Forster and Forster 1996 pg. 72).

6 December 1824

"I immediately had Jean and Lucain arrested, just as I had said I would, and had them put in leg irons." "My first question is, under what conditions? Monsieur, he replies, you will no longer have any losses on your place, the ravages of poison will stop. I forgave everything, the rogues were set free, but eight of them will be held responsible. At the first sign of trouble, they will be retaken and put into irons for the remainder of their days." "Jean is a great monster, and it appears that he and Marie Barnabe are the most guilty." "In all, we lost twelve mules, ten draft oxen, and three cows or heifers, plus Bibiane killed herself and Roc hanged himself." (Forster and Forster 1996 pg. 73).

"Population increase at the sugar plantation is zero, so that we must figure into our expenses the purchase of eight negroes every year. At the Cafeiere, we have had four births this year, and these children are superb." (Forster and Forster 1996 pg. 73).

"Chignac's departure has now become indispensable, for all our misfortunes were caused by the slaves' hatred for him." (Forster and Forster 1996 pg. 73).

In March 1824 Dessalles is singing the praises of his applied strategy to deal with the enslaved, their productivity, resistance and reproduction on the sugar plantation. By May 1824 he is faced with the need to apply an austerity programme to the enterprise to reduce the operating expenses in a bid to increase profits towards paying off debts that have become due. But there are operating costs that refuse to comply with his strategy the most important being the need to purchase on an annual basis enslaved African labour. The enslaved African labour force is reduced appreciably by disease and suicide and enslaved African labour is not reproducing itself. The refusal of the enslaved Africans to reproduce is a constant dilemma to Dessalles which he never unravels and a most potent indicator of African resistance. By July 1824 Dessalles' much vaunted system of social control collapses as the poisoning of livestock on his plantation now presents the most potent ongoing challenge to his all-powerful stance on the plantation. Dessalles' response to the poisoning assault betrays the weakness of the white minority in dealing with a majority enslaved race in rebellion upon whom the entire capitalist wealth generating machine is hinged. Dessalles applies collective punishment to the entire non house slave population of the sugar plantation. Dessalles is looking for an informer or informers to give up those assaulting his order on the plantation. In September 1824, 30 of the enslaved escaped from the plantation were rounded up and returned with Jean receiving 100 lashes a grave failure of Dessalles' policing and security mechanisms. The informer, Jean-Pierre came forward and Dessalles now completed his rogues list in September 1824 but he refuses to kill, to take the lives of the rogues choosing instead to place them in chains and include them in the work force. He then boasts that the entire enslaved work force surrendered to him led by Jean where a détente was worked out where in exchange for the removal of the chains from the rogues and the end of the collective punishment the assault on his power will end. Which Dessalles touted as his great victory but the suicides continued and Dessalles needed to purchase enslaved labour on an annual basis. The grave reality for Dessalles is his inability to kill labour that he desperately needed to keep the capitalist enterprise going especially in a period of austerity. He simply could not have afforded to make public spectacles of the executions of those who mounted the assault on white power in his plantation. Wealth generation, given his families' level of demand on the cash generated by the plantation was his primary concern, hence the embrace of the détente.

Dessalles was before July 1824 convinced that his order was threatened externally of the plantation and in response heightened the isolation of the enslaved of his plantation from those of the surrounding plantations. The case of Eusebe destroyed his trust in the efficacy of the bubble he placed the plantation in. The case of the assault from within then left Dessalles' order in tatters forcing him to create scapegoats to blame the failure of his experiment on. In this case it was the free Mulattoes and Chignac. Dessalles' racism lured him into underestimating the nature of the challenge to his power the enslaved Africans were willing to mount. Dessalles actually believed that his strategy to manage the power relations with the enslaved was actually working to place him in a hegemonic position which will not be effectively challenged as he had seduced them all into accepting their enslavement and the need to work hard to generate wealth for Dessalles. The reality which revealed itself in September left Dessalles no choice but to accept détente which was a position that contradicted the hegemonic discourse of slavery which made capital punishment mandatory for acts of rebellion as those of Jean. This system failure was the product of his racism where he simply could not accept that an inferior race will mount an effective challenge repeatedly to his power and dominance and act upon this reality. The constant resistance of the enslaved Africans and the demands of an export driven capitalist enterprise in an operational environment devoid of an effective State form were the demise of this hybrid experiment. Powerlessness drives Dessalles to détente and the framing of scapegoats. For the continued instability on the plantation can impact his ability to continue to be an investable entity on the part of the merchant houses of France. With the loss of cash advances to fund the operations of the plantation to facilitate raw sugar production from the merchants the enterprise collapses. The enterprise was then not in a state to generate capital savings towards investing in the enterprise to reduce debt financing. The market value of the raw sugar exported to the metropole, the volume of annual production, the costs of production and especially the drawings from the cash flow of the enterprise to fund the lifestyle of the family all conspired to create vulnerable plantation capitalism rooted in enslavement. The enterprise and the white owners/beneficiaries lived on credit, which was driven by the sense of white entitlement manifested in the life of lavish luxury and indolence made possible by African enslavement, justified by the discourse of white racist supremacy.

What is most obvious from the 1824 letters of Dessalles is the operational existence of power relations on the Dessalles plantation in spite of African enslavement. The capitalist basis of production of raw sugar for export to markets in the metropole ensured that capitalist relations of production be present and demand power relations between enslaved /worker and owner of the enterprise /massa. In addition, this capitalist entity was part of a globalised capitalist circuit which embraced the metropole, the Caribbean, West Africa and North America and was a key factor in the rise of industrial capitalism in Britain and France. The capitalist plantation order was then at best schizoid where massa/owner was called upon to contest force/domination/violence relations and power relations with the enslaved/workers. Where the power relations demanded by capitalist production was at odds with the violence/domination/force relations of the hegemonic discourse of enslavement. Dessalles then chose to formulate his own specific blend in the hope of seducing the enslaved to be productive workers reproducing labour in spite of their enslavement and the enslavement they were condemning their children to. By insisting that the violence/force/domination will be always present but in the background where its use will be determined by the discipline of the enslaved /workers. But in 1824 public potent resistance scuttled the tentative peace. The word was poison!

In the letters of 1824 the reality emerges of the divisions within the enslaved where Dessalles is loud in praise for his house slaves for having provided a safe haven for him on the plantation especially in times of instability. It is apparent from previous letters that Dessalles' strategy calls for the constituting of slaves throughout the ranks of the enslaved where slaves identify with the agenda of the owner/massa rather than with resistance which has a race identity. The manufactured dichotomy of house slave vs. field slave simply did not exist on the Dessalles plantation for the assets of Dessalles existed throughout the population of the enslaved on the plantation. Disciplined, self-policed, internalisation of white racist discourse with its anti-African intent, self-hate and viewing the world through white racist discourse. The condition of black skin, white masks. This sums up the individual constituted by white racist supremacist discourse which was the means to divide the enslaved where informers, hand wringers and the hopeless destroy all attempts at resistance.

This model will proliferate under the post Emancipation colonial state where in the era of independence the State was handed over to this group crucial to facilitate the neo-colonial order.

1825

22 January 1825

"On the first of the year, the negroes poisoned one of my oxen as a New Year's present," "they poisoned a second one, and I found chains on all the rogues who had been taken out of them on 25 September last. Since then, everything is going well; the hospital is empty," (Forster and Forster 1996 pg. 74).

"The plantation is in magnificent condition, and we will bring in big revenues. All it takes is order and thrift. They will get tired of doing evil, and we will have a few more years of tranquillity." (Forster and Forster 1886 pg. 74).

1 February 1825

"Do you realise that those who are in chains are our most valuable subjects?"

18 February 1825

"It is generally believed this time that the poison comes from the free people of colour, who are giving evil advice to the slaves." "It was no doubt a plot, and everything seems to point to perfidious plans, but we have nothing to fear." (Forster and Forster 1996 pg. 75).

27 February 1825

"Since 1 February, we have lost three draft oxen, a little calf, and a small heifer." "Moise, who was in chains, threw himself into the big vat just as it came to the boil. He was pulled out and died 24 hours later. He confessed to things that make your hair stand on end. Jean is dead. I believe that he communicated with somebody during the night and they smuggled in some poison with which he killed himself." (Forster and Forster 1996 pg. 75).

"The losses continue. All the plantations are in the same situation, and it is believed that the free mulattoes incite the slaves." (Forster and Forster 1996 pg. 75).

15 April 1825

"because any talk of poison would have caused the Europeans, who have only a very imperfect understanding of our colonies, to imagine that everything was lost, everything was desperate." (Forster and Forster 1996 pg. 76).

"But that presupposes the government's will to preserve the colonies, and to give them a little better protection than in the past." (Forster and Forster 1996 pg. 76).

10 May 1825

"On the agenda is the decision concerning three ships accused of having engaged in the slave trade. General Donzelot is vigorously pursuing the slave ship owners. Our greatest enemies are some persons in the administration, even though these people owe their fortunes to the colonies." (Forster and Forster 1996 pg. 76).

"At every execution decreed by the provost court, we see free men of colour executed, along with a lot of unclaimed recaptured runaways, an extremely dangerous class of people that is increasing in an alarming manner." (Forster and Forster 1996 pg. 77).

"Manumissions are no longer authorised since the affair of the mulattoes," (Forster and Forster 1996 pg.77).

22 August 1825

"The news of the independence of Saint-Domingue has been devastating to the entire white population of these colonies." (Forster and Forster 1996 pg. 78).

5 January 1826

"The poison has not been entirely stopped at our place," "But what is terribly upsetting is to see entire families of whites disappear." (Forster and Forster 1996 pg. 78).

The poison attacks on the Dessalles plantation have not ended in 1826 in spite of his strategy deployed which indicates that the attempt to isolate the enslaved on the Dessalles plantation from the reality external of the plantation has failed. His détente has also failed to seduce specific leaders of the resistance movement into acceptance of the life he has prescribed for them. Moise throws himself into the boiling vat of sugar cane juice which means he was in chains working in the sugar factory sending a most powerful message then confessed and died. Jean again in revolt poisoned himself and died. Both by their suicides providing momentum to the resistance. Dessalles recognises in 1825 that the most valuable members of the enslaved workforce are in chains now two are dead by their own hands. The operational logic of enslavement cannot satisfy the operational demands of a capitalist enterprise whose sole purpose is sustainable wealth generation. Slavery limits the capacity of the capitalist enterprise to fully evolve its wealth generating capacity, it holds capitalism in a parasitic cocoon which spawns a lumpen capitalism with its lumpen bourgeoisie generating lumpen development/underdevelopment.

And specific members of the enslaved simply don't tire of resistance. What is apparent from Dessalles' letters of 1825/26 is the reality that the slave order in Martinique was in ferment as a result of collapse of segments of it. The number of unclaimed runaways being killed by the state illustrates a slave order losing control over the enslaved and now resorting to killing valuable labour power in an attempt to neutralise a feared potent threat. The free non-whites were in a state of active resistance and the state was killing members of this group in an attempt to neutralise another potent threat. The prohibition of the manumission of slaves in the colony was another potent indication of this fear. The colonial state was then reacting to the fear of the replication of the model of the Haitian Revolution in the colony. Supported by Dessalles' morbid fear of France's recognition of the right of Haiti to exist as an independent nation and its impact on Martinique.

The pure brutality of enslavement and the power it exerted to grind you into the dust is potently illustrated by the case of Honore the enslaved. Honore served the mother of Dessalles and was transported to France to continue this service. Honore was sent back to the Dessalles plantation in Martinique where he was assigned to work. Whilst on the plantation Dessalles' mother gave Honore his freedom/gave him his body but Dessalles never revealed the fact although being a magistrate of long standing that the transaction was null and void in Martinique. Honore was unable to register his free paper and remained an enslaved worker on the Dessalles' plantation where he was moved into the residence of Dessalles. As Dessalles' attitude to Honore suddenly changed for the better. Collective punishment designed to break your spirit and destroy your humanity. Note the descriptive term for manumission: to give him/her their body. View the blood-letting even lust of the Haitian Revolution in light of this. A technology of power later revived, reformulated and applied by Nazi Germany, Apartheid South Africa and Apartheid Israel.

Dessalles in 1825/26 continues to rail against the colonial government, its officials and the metropolitan state in spite of being a long standing member of the judiciary of Martinique. He states that Europeans simply cannot understand the nature of the colony of Martinique as they would insist that the spate of poisonings was the end of the colony as a viable business proposition. There is then a perceptual inability of Europeans to understand and act in the interest of the colonies which ensures that the metropolitan state and the colonial government and its officials are unable to act in the interests of the colony. Dessalles offers no solution. Dessalles' position on the prosecution of slave runners by the State and the recognition of free non-whites as free persons indicate the nature of the problem he had with government which was a problem of the rule of law when it impinged on white entitlement. France was a signatory to the articles of the Congress of Vienna 1815 which outlawed the slave trade. Dessalles had a problem with policing this treaty as it impacted the slave trade to the colony and the interests of the slave owners. This treaty obligation must not be policed as it damaged white entitlement. Dessalles considered the free non-whites as the gravest threat to the slave order of society as he conceived it as a race order where free non-whites were an aberration. To recognise free non-whites as free was in effect destroying the race/slave order and the very economy of the colony. The laws which did so must then be silenced to protect white entitlement.

It is then apparent from the letters of Pierre Dessalles considered, white racist supremacy had placed the colony in a time warp where developments in France with reference to the nature of hegemonic bourgeois scientific discourse had rendered colonial discourse practically unintelligible. Dessalles was shouting across a roaring discursive chasm to a hegemonic discursive citadel whose political imperatives impacted the colony not the obverse. Slavery in existence in the colony in 1826 is as a result of the politics of France not the politics of the slave order of the colony. And when the politics of France shifted again in 1848 slavery was its casualty whilst Dessalles was simply a passive recipient. The hegemonic discourse of African enslavement of Martinique was at best a subjugated knowledge in the discursive terrain of France in 1825/26. This subjugated knowledge then supplied inputs to the formulation of technologies of power to exert power over colonies in the post enslavement era and over non-white migrant communities in France, the legacies of empire.

Conclusion

What is obvious from this deconstruction is that both Mary Nugent and Pierre Dessalles both saw the need to modify the hegemonic discourse of African enslavement necessary to ensuring the sustainability of the slave economy and acted upon their belief. But the politics of the colonies, essentially of maintaining the hegemony of a white powered minority over an enslaved non-white majority and the politics of the metropole erected potent limits to the quest for a new discourse of slavery. The Haitian Revolution 1804 deeply impacted the politics of the slave order of Jamaica and Martinique triggering a state of permanent fear of white genocide at the hands of the African enslaved which drove the knee jerk reaction to brutality driven by racist paranoia. And the enslaved willingly acted upon white paranoia as it heightened the potency of the resistance of those intent on resistance. The politics of white paranoia came at the worst political juncture for the white oligarchy of the slave colonies as the metropole was in the grip of the hegemony of bourgeois discourse. In its application of the two technologies of power clothed in the public discourse of law and sovereignty the capitalist enterprise rooted in enslavement was now problematic. The pre-bourgeois discourse of law and sovereignty in its bourgeois reformulation in the nineteenth century and thereafter now made enslavement a political issue. An instrument of the old order with its politics that the bourgeois was intent on flushing away. To attack enslavement was to attack the interests of an order marked for absorption and eclipse. A strategic assault was necessary as hegemonic discourse in the slave colonies was incongruous with bourgeois hegemonic discourse in Europe and nowhere in Europe was this more apparent than in Britain of the 1830's which is illustrated by the records of those slave owners compensated by the British State for the loss of their property with the abolition of slavery. In Britain this process was rolled out in the decade of the 1830s in France it was rolled out in the 1790s by the revolutionary government, reversed by the swing to the right with the coup d'état of Napoleon Bonaparte and thereafter and in 1848 with the coup d'état of the Republicans, the end of the monarchists and the abolition of slavery. The politics of the metropole destroyed the slave order and the politics of the slave colonies did everything in their power to confirm to the politicians of the metropole that the end of the slave order was good politics. The discourse of white racist supremacy, the product of the slave order then held the social order in stasis that isolated it and rendered it unintelligible from/to the evolution of politics in the metropole. But the legacy bequeathed to the North Atlantic, the discourse of white racist supremacy is absorbed, reformulated and repeatedly redeployed in the North Atlantic from the nineteenth to the twenty-first centuries. In its twenty-first century redeployment the discourse of racist white supremacy of the North Atlantic will be familiar to Mary Nugent and Pierre Dessalles. The twenty-first century redeployment is an allusion to National Socialism and fascist discourses, what it is in composition and worldview is a resurrection, tailoring and redeployment of nineteenth century West Indian white racist supremacy in the twenty-first century with neo-liberal austere capitalism and its assault on workers attached.

For my analyses of the legacy of racism in the West Indies see:

https://www.daurius.com/caribbean-social-order

https://www.daurius.com/books

References

Forster, Elborg and Forster, Robert (1996): "Sugar and Slavery, Family and Race the letters and diary of Pierre Dessalles, planter in Martinique 1808-1856" John Hopkins University Press USA

Foucault, Michel (2003): "Society Must Be Defended Lectures at the College de France 1975-1976" Picador USA

Foucault, Michel (1990): "The History of Sexuality Volume 1: An Introduction" Vintage Books USA

Wright, Philip (ed.) (2002): "Lady Nugent's Journal of her residence in Jamaica from 1801 to 1805" UWI Press Jamaica

Also by Daurius Figueira

Discourse of Slavery

Massa's White Supremacist Discourse of West Indian Negro Slavery
Deconstructed Volume 1
Massa's White Supremacist Discourse of West Indian Negro Slavery
Deconstructed Volume 2

Frantz Fanon for the 21st Century

Frantz Fanon for the 21st Century Volume 1 Frantz Fanon's Discourse of
Racism and Culture, the Negro and the Arab Deconstructed
Frantz Fanon for the 21st Century Volume 2 Frantz Fanon's Discourse of
Decolonisation and Violence, the Nature of Power and Power Relations of
Neo-colonial African States,
Frantz Fanon for the 21st Century Volume 3 The Algerian Revolution, Islamic
Discourse, the Colonizer and the Discourse of White Supremacy

Standalone

Belize: Human Smuggling, Transnational Organised Crime, Politicians And
Public Servants
Biopower, Racism, State Racism and The Modern/Post Modern North
Atlantic State: Michel Foucault's Genealogy of the Historico-Political
Discourse of Race War Deconstructed

Derek Walcott's Poetry Deconstructed, Its Political and Sociological Discourse Revealed

Transnational Organized Crime and Drug Trafficking in the Second Decade of the 21st Century in the Dominican Republic, Suriname, Venezuela, French Guiana, Martinique and Guadeloupe

The Islamic State and the Muslims of Trinidad and Tobago in the 21st Century

A Deconstruction of Michel Foucault's 1979 Discourse of Neo-Liberalism for the 21st Century

A Deconstruction of Qu'ranic Discourse for the 21st Century

Watch for more at https://www.daurius.com.

About the Author

Daurius Figueira is a researcher, analyst and author located in the anti-Enlightenment and anti-Science discourse/worldview/paradigm specialising in the study of the illicit drug trade, the illicit small arms trade and human smuggling of the Caribbean, Islamic extremism and racism/white supremacy with an emphasis on power relations. You can access his website to experience and download his research papers published online and view his range of books. His website address is: https://www.daurius.com and his blog on the Caribbean is at: https://drugtrade.wordpress.com/

Read more at https://www.daurius.com.